PRAISE FOR *SOMETHING FOR THE PAIN*

'Fascinating…Totally intriguing, utterly hilarious.'
Gideon Haigh, *Offsiders*

'Murnane's way of being interested in horse racing
is like no one else's.' Owen Richardson, *Age*

'This is Murnane, the stylist, at his best…An unusual book
by an unusual man.' Les Carlyon, *Australian*

'*Something for the Pain* is not about great events.
It is, however, a great read.' *Inside Racing*

'There is much here for those who adore Murnane's
writing…It is perhaps his biggest gamble, and he
has won it.' Scott Esposito, *Lifted Brow*

'Bears testament to a lifelong obsession and further illustrates
the breadth and depth of meaningfulness that Murnane can
draw from a seemingly straightforward spectacle.'
Shannon Burns, *Australian Book Review*

'A memoir of horse racing that speaks of triumphs and
tragedies, of the infinite shades of friendship and romance.'
Paul Griffiths, *Times Literary Supplement* Books of the Year

'If Australian writing were a horse race, Murnane
would be the winner by three and a half lengths.'
Andy Griffiths

Shortlisted, 2015 Victorian Premier's Literary Awards

Gerald Murnane was born in Melbourne in 1939 and spent part of his childhood in country Victoria. He has been a primary teacher, an editor, and a university lecturer. His debut novel, *Tamarisk Row*, was followed by nine other works of fiction, the most recent of which is *A Million Windows*. He has also published a collection of non-fiction pieces, *Invisible Yet Enduring Lilacs*. Murnane has won the Patrick White Award, the Melbourne Prize for Literature, and the Adelaide Festival Award for Innovation. He lives in western Victoria.

SOMETHING FOR THE PAIN

Something for the Pain

A Memoir of
the Turf

Gerald Murnane

Text Publishing Melbourne Australia

textpublishing.com.au

The Text Publishing Company
Swann House
22 William Street
Melbourne Victoria 3000
Australia

First published in 2015 by The Text Publishing Company
An earlier version of the first section appeared in *Seizure*
Reprinted 2015

Cover & page design by W. H. Chong
Typeset in Granjon by J & M Typesetting

Printed in Australia by Griffin Press, an Accredited ISO AS/NZS 14001:2004 Environmental Management System printer

National Library of Australia Cataloguing-in-Publication entry

ISBN: 9781925240375 (paperback)

ISBN: 9781922253187 (ebook)

Creator: Murnane, Gerald, 1939– author.

Title: Something for the pain : a memoir of the turf / by Gerald Murnane.

Subjects: Murnane, Gerald, 1939–. Authors, Australian—Biography.
Horse racing.

Dewey Number: 798.40092

 This book is printed on paper certified against the Forest Stewardship Council® Standards. Griffin Press holds FSC chain-of-custody certifi-cation SGS-COC-005088. FSC promotes environmentally responsible, socially beneficial and economically viable management of the world's forests.

1. *Something for the Pain*

MACHINERY AND TECHNOLOGY have always intimidated me. I did not dare to use a motor mower until I was in my fifties with sons old enough to help me start it. I bought a mobile phone fifteen years ago and have carried it ever since in the boot of my car. I make a call occasionally but have never even learned to store numbers in my machine. My previous car had a facility for playing audio tapes, and I succeeded in mastering it. However, the car that I bought four years ago plays only compact discs. I have a few discs that I listen to occasionally at home but not enough to warrant my struggling with the thing in my dashboard. I can use the radio in my car but, because I live in a remote district, I can pick up only a few stations and their programs fail to interest me. Luckily, I can pick up the station that broadcasts horse races from all over Australia and even, sometimes, from New Zealand. I still call the station 3UZ, although it acquired a fancy new name some years ago.

Only a few years ago, the *Herald Sun* published every day the fields and riders and form for every race meeting covered by the Victorian TAB. Nowadays, only a few meetings appear in print. No doubt the details of all the other meetings are available on some or another website, but a man who can't use the CD player in his car is hardly likely to be able to use computers. And so, when I'm driving on some lonely road in the far west of Victoria and I switch on my car radio, the names of the horses in the race being described are likely to be names that I've never seen in print. The course where the race is being run is likely to be far away in the vast part of Australia where I've never been. What, then, do I see in mind while I'm listening to a rapidly delivered report of the changing positions of horses unknown to me in a place I've seen only on maps?

Writing has for me at least one advantage over speaking. While I'm writing, I pause often to make sure that the words I'm about to set down are truly accurate. I may have told someone in conversation that I often see in mind, while I'm driving alone, a field of horses approaching a winning post at Gunnedah or Rockhampton or Northam. But I'm not about to write that I see any such thing. I ought rather to write that a radio broadcast of a horse race brings to my mind a swarm of vague, blurred images, a few being images of horses with jockeys up but most having no resemblance to horses or jockeys. The images are accompanied by feelings, some easy to report—such as my willing one or another horse to win—and others difficult indeed to describe.

Perhaps if I were a horseman, I would more easily call to mind the horses themselves while I listen to race broadcasts. I might even imagine the race from the viewpoint of a jockey with a straining, pounding horse beneath him. The fact is, though, that I've never sat astride a horse, let alone urged it into a gallop or even a canter. During all the countless hours that I've spent on racecourses, I've never really looked at a horse. When I recall some of the famous horses that have raced in front of me—Tulloch, Tobin Bronze, Vain, Kingston Town, and the like—I see in mind no images of bays or browns or chestnuts or whatever, with distinctive heads or confor- mation. Instead, I might recall, for example, the finish of the first race that Tulloch won in Melbourne, on Caulfield Cup Day, 1956, or the newspaper pictures of his elderly owner during the weeks when the old fool dithered over Tulloch's running in the 1957 Melbourne Cup. I would not fail to see an image of Tulloch's racing colours— Red-and-white striped jacket, black sleeves and cap. I would see also the features of the jockey who often rode Tulloch, Neville Sellwood, the same man who deliberately stopped Tulloch from winning the 1960 Melbourne Cup, just as he stopped the favourite, Yeman, from winning the 1958 Cup. (I can't prove these claims, but for me they are facts of history.) As well as seeing these things in mind, I would feel again the feelings forever bound up with those remembered images. I might even become again for a moment the troubled young man that I was when Tulloch was racing. But I don't want to go *there* just now. I'm supposed to be writing about my present self, alone in my car on an empty road and hearing a report of a field of unknown horses on some faraway racecourse.

Many people seem to believe that what passes through their minds is a sort of mental film: a replay of things that have already happened or of things that might happen in the future. Perhaps some people do have films running through their minds, but most of the sequences in my mind are more like cartoons or comic strips or surreal paintings. Often, the sounds of a race broadcast will cause me to see in mind what I saw during the first years when I heard such sounds. Those were the years from 1944 to 1948, when I lived in a weatherboard cottage in Neale Street, Bendigo. I would have liked, during those years, to sit in the kitchen with my father of a Saturday afternoon and to listen with him to the radio broadcasts of races from Flemington, Caulfield, Moonee Valley, or Mentone, but both my parents discouraged me from doing so. If they sensed already that their eldest child was on the way to becoming obsessed with horse racing, then they were absolutely correct. If they sensed that he would one day gamble recklessly, crazily, on horses as his father was often apt to gamble, then they were wrong. And if they thought that their banning him from listening to race broadcasts would take away his interest in horse racing, then they were likewise wrong.

Bendigo was a quiet place in the mid-1940s. Few motor vehicles passed along Neale Street or nearby McIvor Road. Even halfway down the backyard, among my pretend-landscapes of farms and roads and townships each with a racecourse on its outskirts—even there I could hear as much as I needed to hear of the sounds from the mantel radio in the kitchen. What I heard were not distinctive words but vocal sounds: a chant or a recitative that began quietly, progressed evenly, rose to a climax, and then subsided again. I had never seen a horse race, but I saw every Wednesday the centre pages of the *Sporting Globe*. That thriving publication was always printed on pink newsprint, which made the dim reproductions of black-and-white photographs even more grey and grainy. The centre pages of the *Globe*, as everyone called it, were filled with results of the Melbourne race meeting of the previous Saturday. Around the margins were detailed statistics, and on either side of the central gutter were the pictures that I pored over: two pictures for every race, one of the field at the home turn and the other of the same field at the winning post.

The pictures, as I wrote above, were grey and grainy. As well, several of the racecourses of Melbourne were so arranged that the winning post was overshadowed by the grandstands from mid-afternoon onwards. As a result, anyone wanting to see in the *Globe* the images of the horses themselves had to strain to distinguish them from the murky background. This never troubled me. I learned all that I wanted to learn from the names of the horses, which were clearly printed in uppercase letters in the upper half of each illustration. Each name was enclosed in a boldly outlined rectangle, and from some part of the lower margin of each rectangle a shape like a curved stalactite led down to the head of the horse denoted by the name in the rectangle.

I recall still, nearly seventy years later, some of the first racehorse names that I read in the *Sporting Globe*. More than that, I recall the effect on me of my reciting those names in the way that the racing commentators recited them. So strongly do I recall the effects of some names that I am able nowadays to put out of my mind the dictionary meanings of those names and to see the clusters of images that they promoted long ago and to feel the moods connected with the images. I did not know, for example, the dictionary meaning of the word HIATUS or even whether the word was to be found in any dictionary. Whenever I saw the word above the blurred image of a racehorse in the *Globe*, I saw at once an image of a bird in flight above a deserted seashore or estuary. Not until many years later did I learn who were the ICENE or who was TAMERLANE. The word ICENE above the blurred image of a racehorse brought to mind a long silver-white robe worn by some notable female personage and the pleasant sound of the train of the robe as it swept across a floor of cream-coloured marble. TAMERLANE denoted for me a grassy pathway overhung by rows of tamarisk trees. Many names, however, failed to impress me or even repelled me. (It seemed to me then, and it seems still, that most racehorses are poorly named.) I can recall from the 1940s such drab names as LORD BADEN, CHEERY BOY, and ZEZETTE. The bearers of such names fared badly in my early imaginary races, which were invariably won by horses with appealing names.

I have hardly begun to describe the complexity of what I saw and felt during those imaginary races. Vague shapes of horses were in the background, but the foreground included more than names in uppercase letters and the imagery arising from those names. Hovering nearby were shadowy images of persons, most of them men in suits and ties and with grey felt hats low on their brows.

In the 1940s, and for several decades afterwards, racehorses in Australia were owned usually by one man alone, and all trainers and jockeys were men. Nowadays, syndicates predominate, many with ten or more members, but I grew up believing that the typical owner of a horse racing in Melbourne was a wealthy businessman or grazier, or a medical or legal practitioner. The typical trainer may have lacked the social standing of the owners, his clients, but he looked hardly different, and if he was one of those described by racing journalists as *shrewd* or *astute* he might have been even wealthier than they. Since no well-dressed or wealthy men were to be seen in the back streets of Bendigo, the image-men in my mind must have been derived from illustrations in newspapers. As for the men's histories or personalities, I seemed to have understood already that these were of little account on a racecourse; an owner or a trainer was defined by the performance of his horses.

My image-horses had image-jockeys, but these were mostly inscrutable. The nearest I had come to seeing an actual jockey was my standing beside my father at the Bendigo Showgrounds on a cold evening during the Easter Fair while a few harness horses paraded before the race that was run as part of a program of foot races and cycling races and axemen's contests. My father called out to a driver that he knew, and the man walked his horse to the outside fence, leaned back in his sulky, and exchanged a few words. While horse and driver were approaching us, my father had told me that the driver was Clarry Long and the horse Great Dalla. Clarry, like many Bendigonians, was of Chinese descent and his mostly expressionless demeanour made him seem to me more self-assured than myself or my father. Clarry was wearing the first set of racing colours that I had seen, and the same weak light from atop the nearby stanchion that made his face seem waxen worked also on the satin of his jacket. I have for long surmised that Great Dalla's colours were Brown, pale-blue stars and cap, but such was the play of light on the star shapes, on that long-ago evening in faraway Bendigo, that I sometimes decide that the stars on the brown background were not pale blue but silver or even mauve or lilac.

The meagre details reported in the previous half-dozen paragraphs all went into the making of the complex imagery that appeared to me whenever I heard from the backyard the sounds of a race broadcast. At different times while the chanted sounds reached me, I was aware of images of greyish-pink horse shapes, of horse names in uppercase letters, of spectators looking out anxiously from under hat brims, of jockeys with mask-like faces and vague-coloured jackets. I was aware, too, that much was at stake while these images jostled and vied.

The human voice is a marvellous instrument, and the ear that interprets it is hardly less so. I seem to have learned during my first days as a listener to race broadcasts that a caller is sometimes able to signal to his listeners, even when the field is a hundred metres or more from the winning post, that one or another horse will almost certainly win. In some such races the likely winner may have broken clear from the rest; in many a race it may be some distance behind the leaders but gaining noticeably. Whatever the situation, the caller is able to utter the relevant name with such emphasis that his listeners are spared any further suspense. In the dusty backyard, I was often unable to make out a single name but still able to detect the emphatic utterance that signalled in advance the result of a race and to hope that the name thus emphasised was one that I would have deemed worthy.

Driving alone nowadays and hearing reports of the progress of horses unknown to me, I often choose from a number of names the one that most appeals to me. I then suppose myself to be one of the owners of the horse so named or to have backed it to win a large sum. Then I listen intently, hoping to hear my chosen name uttered with the certain emphasis that I learned, nearly seventy years ago, to recognise. On one such occasion recently, the invisible horse that I aligned myself with had a name that appealed to me greatly but the horse itself was always toiling at the rear, to use one of the many stock expressions of race callers and racing journalists.

Even as a dreaming child, I had no wish to be a caller of races. I must have understood that I could never be cool enough or impartial enough during the running of a race to be able to report its developments accurately. And yet, I've been for most of my life moved often to hear in mind or to whisper under my breath or even, sometimes when alone, to deliver aloud a few phrases or a single word from a broadcast of some or another race never yet run on Earth. I was thus moved on the occasion mentioned above, after the horse with the appealing name had finished among the tailenders. I was driving at the time on a back road with bitumen wide enough for only one vehicle. I would have felt at liberty to express myself not just once but several times, except that I saw from the rear-vision mirror that a huge truck was close behind me. Apparently I had slowed down while I was preoccupied with racing matters, and the driver of the truck was now anxious for me to get back to the speed limit or to pull over into the gravel and let him pass.

I saw just then a signpost ahead on the left and I flicked on my left-side blinker. The road that I turned into was of gravel and overhung with trees. I guessed that it led towards the Little Desert but the paddocks on either side were well grassed and dotted with sheep. I found a place wide enough for a safe U-turn and stopped. I wound down the driver's-side window. I listened at first to the profound silence. Then I drew a deep breath and cried out once only what I had been urged for some time past to cry out. Then I watched perhaps a dozen sheep on the far side of the fence lift their heads and stare in my direction. I waited until every sheep had resumed its grazing and then I cried out again—not to the sheep but to the ideal listeners in the ideal world that I first postulated nearly seventy years ago when I first heard a disembodied voice cry out with significant emphasis some such name as *Something for the Pain*.

2. The Drunk in the Dance Hall

I COULD NEVER learn to dance. At different times during the 1950s my mother, my first girlfriend, and the instructors employed by two separate schools of ballroom dancing all tried to teach me, but to no avail. I am not by nature a clumsy person, yet somehow the effort to place my feet in the correct positions while holding a female person at close quarters and conducting with her an inter-mittent conversation—somehow, all this was too much for me. I went to a few dances as a young man and even dared sometimes to dance with some or another young female person. What am I saying? I never *danced* with anyone. I stumbled and tottered and tried to bluff my way around the dance floor, all the while praying for the music to stop, and I remain to this day grateful to the few young women, whoever they were, who glided backwards in front of me, keeping out of reach of my clodhopping feet.

I dared thus sometimes but mostly I preferred to lurk near the rear of the dance hall with the other young males who were reluctant or unable to dance. I knew that we were the male equivalents of wallflowers: those young women who sat through a dance because no one had claimed them as partners. Perhaps I even understood that we were cowards by comparison—the young women sat bravely alone while we males tried to hide ourselves in a pack. I wonder whether I sometimes tried to appear to be in earnest conversation with one of my companions, as though we had serious matters to settle before returning to the frivolity of the dance floor.

Nearly twenty years before my birth, my father hung about the rear of dance halls and, on one occasion at least, he had an earnest conversation with another of his kind. The previous sentence is perhaps misleading. My father's interlocutor was like him in being a reluctant dancer but quite unlike him in being drunk. (My father was a lifelong abstainer.) Perhaps the other man had been drunk when he arrived at the dance, or perhaps some of the young men present had been drinking beer or spirits in the darkness outside the hall, as would have happened often in the country district where my father grew up. Regardless of what or where the man had been drinking, he must have been drunk indeed to have discussed what he discussed with my father at the rear of the dance hall.

I am writing not history but a batch of recollected impressions and daydreams. With only a single statistic to support me, I mention here one of the most noticeable changes in racing during my lifetime. From about the 1960s, when off-course totalisator betting was legalised and became widespread, the number of on-course bookmakers has dwindled and such expressions as 'beating the bookmaker' have become outmoded. Things were different indeed during my youth and, from what I've read and heard, things were mightily different before my time. I looked just now into the race book that I bought for two shillings on the cold day in June 1964 when I went to the races at Caulfield with the young woman who later became my wife. On the pages listing the bookmakers betting that day, 266 names appear. At the equivalent meeting this year, perhaps a tenth of that number might be counted.

The scale of betting seems also to have declined. Legalised off-course betting greatly increased the revenue of the racing clubs and more than compensated for the loss of gate takings from the smaller crowds. Much of the increased revenue went into the prize money paid to owners of winners and placed horses. For many years now, successful owners have been able to recoup a large part of their expenses from prize money alone. In the 1960s and earlier, the only way for an owner to show a profit was by betting. I knew a small-time owner in the 1950s who bet two hundred pounds on his horse whenever it started in a race. This was a very modest bet for an owner of those days, and yet its equivalent in today's money would be more than ten thousand dollars. When one of the leading stables was confident of the chances of one of their horses, owner, trainer and stable followers would organise a so-called plunge. Commission agents well known to leading bookmakers would descend on the ring at a pre-arranged time and would place credit bets of hundreds or even thousands of pounds all at once and before the bookmakers could reduce their odds. In the great days of betting, the chief concern of the connections of a horse was to obtain the highest possible odds on the day when it stood the best chance of winning. Many a horse was 'set' for some or another race months in advance. The stewards did their best to ensure that every horse ran always on its merits or 'tried', but in most races the also-rans included horses that were 'cold' or 'dead'—their jockeys were under instructions to have them finish in the ruck so that bookmakers would bet lucrative odds against them on the day when the owner, the trainer, and those in the know launched their plunge and the horse was at last allowed to show its true ability.

F. H. Slamen (Brown, yellow stripes and cap) owned a chain of newsagencies in the 1950s and also numerous racehorses that were spread among several trainers. It was said of Mr Slamen that he wanted his horses either to win or to run last. A typical horse bearing the brown and the yellow might start five or six times over a period of many months, finishing always well back. Then, with no warning, the same horse would one day be backed off the map, as the saying had it. To use another racecourse expression, they jumped out of trees to back the horse (meaning that they had been hiding beforehand in the foliage to avoid being seen by bookmakers who, if they had got wind of a plunge, would have offered much-reduced odds).

The bookmakers, of course, did not meekly await form reversals and fierce plunges. Leading bookmakers paid for information from track watchers at morning gallops and, according to rumour, from stable spies or disaffected employees. Trainers resorted to counter measures. Ray McLaren (Red, white sash and cap, blue sleeves), an astute trainer from Mentone, needing to give a certain horse one last trial against the clock before a betting tilt, took the horse—Fordell, I think it was—all the way to Pakenham and galloped it at noon on the deserted track.

My father often assured me that racing was even more noted for its plots and intrigues during his heyday, which ran from the early 1920s until the late 1930s. Small wonder, then, that he sat patiently beside a young drunk one night at the rear of a dance hall in the south-west of Victoria and pieced together the details of an elaborate plan. A certain horse from the Warrnambool district, a jumper with poor form, was going to be taken by rail to Sydney in a few weeks and be backed there at long odds to win a steeplechase. (Jumps races were still run in New South Wales at that time.) The rest of the story is easily told. My father travelled himself to Sydney and won several hundred pounds on the horse. (This was more than he could have earned in a year from the labouring jobs that he then worked at.) Yes, this much is easily told, and my father told it to me often, but I can only guess at the more interesting details. Who was the blabbing drunk? I don't care to know his name, but I would dearly like to know how a pie-eyed loudmouth was privy to the plotting of a group of masterminds of the turf. Was he blurting out his precious information into the air around him before my father overheard him, or did he single out my father and whisper to him alone? Was he not dancing because he had arrived at the hall already drunk, or had he become drunk to hide his shyness or his incompetence as a dancer?

I can readily imagine a number of versions of the story, but if I know anything about my father I can state that he would have much preferred to sit and listen to the drunk than to ask some young woman onto the dance floor. Like me, he was hopeless at dancing and ill at ease in female company. Racing was often for him what it has been sometimes for me: a sort of higher vocation excusing us from engaging with the mundane.

3. A Bernborough Finish

I WAS NEVER one for hanging pictures or sticking up posters or postcards. I've always preferred to be surrounded by bare, plain surfaces and to have my desk facing a wall rather than a window. Early in 1982, however, when I was a lecturer in a college of advanced education and had been moved to a new office, I discovered that a part of the wall above my desk was a display board with a supply of drawing pins stuck into it, and after staring at it for a few weeks I went against my usual policy. I was careful and selective. The display board was big enough for thirty or forty postcard-sized pictures, but I pinned up only three and grouped them together with much bare space around them. The first two were portraits: one of Emily Brontë and the other of Marcel Proust. The third was actually two linked scenes, the first showing a field of horses entering the straight, and the second showing the winner of the race and his nearest rivals as they reached the winning post. The race was the T. M. Ahern Memorial Handicap, run at Doomben in Brisbane on 1 June 1946. The total prize money for the race was ten thousand pounds, only two hundred pounds less than for the Melbourne Cup of the same year. The race was run over a distance of about 1320 metres, in today's measurements, and was contested by twenty-seven of the best sprinters in Australia.

Races in Brisbane are run in a clockwise direction, and so my picture of the horses on the home turn was at the right of the picture of the finish. The pictures were blurred reproductions of contemporary newspaper illustrations, but it was enough for me that the names of the chief contenders were printed legibly above them. I knew when I first pinned up the pictures that the straight at Doomben was comparatively short for a metropolitan racecourse. I have since learned that it was about 370 metres in 1946. The picture at the right showed Bernborough in about twentieth place and about thirty-five metres from the leaders. In the picture at the left, Bernborough was passing the post in first place, several metres ahead of the second horse.

The twenty horses that Bernborough passed were not tiring stayers at the end of a gruelling long-distance race but crack sprinters at full gallop. Bernborough did not always win his races in this way, but he did it often enough to give rise to an expression often used by journalists and others for many years afterwards. A racehorse or a sportsperson or even a team achieving victory from a seemingly hopeless position was said to have put up a Bernborough finish.

I worked out of the same office from 1981 until I took early retirement in 1995, by which time my place of employment had become a university. During those years, I sometimes sensed that some or another visitor to my room was puzzled by the odd little group of images huddled together on the otherwise bare wall. To the few who enquired I was pleased to explain that the young woman from Victorian England, the eccentric Frenchman, and the bay stallion from Queensland were equally prominent figures in my private mythology and continued to enrich my life equally.

In a better sort of world, I would not have to write this paragraph, but Bernborough (Orange, purple sleeves, black cap) ✔ has been somewhat forgotten by now, even by followers of racing. He was born a few months after my own birth and died a few weeks before my twenty-first birthday. His birthplace was near Oakey, on the Darling Downs, and he died at Spendthrift Farm in Kentucky. He was a huge animal but was said by his handlers to be unusually placid for a stallion and highly intelligent. The most extraordinary part of his story was that few Australians had heard of him until he was six years old. Until then he raced only at Clifford Park racecourse in Toowoomba, where he won about half of his races. Bernborough's defeats there may have been the result of his having to carry huge weights or of the machinations of his connections. His being confined to Toowoomba came about as a result of suspicions by the controlling body of stewards in Queensland that he was owned not by his purported owner but by a man who had been disqualified for life by Queensland stewards for organising a ring-in at Eagle Farm racecourse in Brisbane. The Queensland stewards refused to allow Bernborough to race anywhere in Queensland; stewards in other states concurred with their Queensland colleagues; the local steward at Toowoomba, however, dissented from the Australia-wide ban and Bernborough had his first twenty starts there.

The impasse was finally resolved when Bernborough was sold at a public auction to Azzalin Romano, a wealthy Sydney restaurant owner. The horse was then transferred to the Sydney stables of Harry Plant, who was himself Queensland-born and had been, as a young man, the buckjumping champion of that state. Bernborough had his first start for Romano and Plant at Canterbury in December 1945. He finished fourth. During the next ten months, he won fifteen consecutive races at the highest level in Sydney, Brisbane, and Melbourne. His winning sequence ended when he finished fifth in the Caulfield Cup in October 1946. At his next start, at Flemington on Derby Day, he broke down during the race and was retired. After being sold and shipped to the United States, he had a highly successful career as a sire.

I have several books about Bernborough in my racing library. I'm grateful to the authors for having compiled a host of details that I could never have discovered myself. But no book and no newspaper article or magazine story that I've read has dealt adequately with Bernborough's defeat in the Caulfield Cup of 1946. Nothing will convince me that Bernborough was beaten on his merits in that race. I still believe what my father assured me nearly sixty years ago was common knowledge among the inner circles of racing, which he had access to in those days: that Bernborough's rider, Athol Mulley, a curse be upon his memory, stopped Bernborough from winning in return for a secret payment from one or more leading bookmakers, who stood to win a fortune if the horse was beaten.

There! I've stated in the public domain what I've brooded over in private for most of my life. No one can sue me. The participants, if such they were, are all dead. I've read all the arguments against my view: Mulley was a victim of circumstances; Bernborough met severe interference in running; the stewards never queried Mulley's riding tactics. The plain fact is that Mulley rode Bernborough in the Caulfield Cup in a manner wholly different from the way he rode the horse on every other occasion when he had a large field to contend with. On every other occasion, Bernborough was saved for one last, mighty finishing run down the outside. In the infamous Caulfield Cup, his rider kept the horse buried in the ruck. To use a coarse expression describing the efforts of jockeys to stop their mounts from winning, Mulley was looking for arses to run into.

Writers intending to compare champion racehorses from different eras inevitably begin by declaring that no reliable means exists for making such comparisons. I won't bother with any such disclaimer. Instead, I'll propose that the person best able to quantify the achievements of racehorses is the handicapper and that the race most suited for comparing the opinions of handicappers is the Melbourne Cup, which has been contested by most of the champions of the Australian turf during the past century and a half. (The previous sentence implies that even the greatest sprinters are not to be called true champions: that no one would dare claim Black Caviar or Vain to be the equal of Phar Lap or Carbine.) In every year since 1861, some or another expert handicapper has assessed the career of each of the numerous entrants in the Melbourne Cup and has allotted to each a weight meant to give it an equal chance with every other. In 1946, soon after Bernborough was entered for the Melbourne Cup of that year, he was allotted the weight equivalent of 67.4 kilos. Only three other horses had previously been allotted a higher weight. Phar Lap was allotted 67.8 kilos in 1931, Carbine was allotted 68.7 in 1891, and The Barb was allotted 72.8 in 1869. Now, a querulous reader might accuse me of begging the question with my next claim, which is that The Barb does not deserve to be included in my comparison. The Barb, known as the Black Demon, was an exceptional horse in his time, but the number of racehorses in the 1860s was not to be compared with the numbers in later decades. The man who gave The Barb his preposterous weight (the horse never actually carried it; he did not contest the Cup of 1869) had never seen the like of The Barb, but no one has since thought it remotely likely that The Barb would have finished twenty and more metres ahead of Carbine in a Melbourne Cup, which is what their comparative weights claim. The next point in my argument, so to call it, is that Phar Lap and Carbine, when they were allotted their huge weights, had each won a Melbourne Cup in the previous year. When Bernborough was awarded his 67.4 kilos, he had *never started* in a Melbourne Cup. If Bernborough *had* won a Melbourne Cup, then the handicapper would surely have handicapped him in the following year as a greater horse than Phar Lap and perhaps even Carbine. But Bernborough did *not* win a Melbourne Cup, the querulous reader cries, and my hearing that cry in my mind has persuaded me to stop calling this paragraph an argument. Why should I try to persuade non-believers, anyway? I'll argue no more. I'll simply explain why I consider Bernborough to be a better horse than Phar Lap.

Bernborough was scratched from the 1946 Melbourne Cup a week before the event. Believing as I do that he would have won the Caulfield Cup comfortably if his rider had allowed him, I have no trouble in supposing that he could have won the Melbourne Cup as well. Assuming that he was entered for the Melbourne Cup of the following year and was allotted a weight a little more than Phar Lap's weight in 1931, then I feel justified in my belief that Bernborough rivals Carbine in being our greatest horse. The querulous reader perhaps needs reminding that Phar Lap and Carbine were both bred in New Zealand, whereas Bernborough was bred in Queensland. I could have saved myself the trouble of writing this and the previous paragraph; I could have asserted without fear of contradiction that Bernborough is the greatest horse ever bred in Australia.

I find it peculiarly satisfying that the year when Bernborough became famous was the same year in which I began to read the *Sporting Globe* and to find in horse racing more than I would ever find in any religious or philosophical system. As corny as it sounds, Bernborough and I were meant for each other. I had searched from the first for pictures of horses that came from behind the leaders to claim victory, and here was a horse who came from behind the whole field. I seem to have been at an early age some sort of contrarian who enjoyed seeing the leader run down; the widespread expectation confounded; the winner come from far back; the champion overcome impossible-seeming circumstances. I have no clear recollection of having done so, but I feel sure that I would have arranged at least once with my glass marbles on the lounge-room mat or my chips of stone on my pretend-racecourse under the lilac bush a race in which the winner came from last at the turn, and would have done this *before* I first heard of Bernborough or saw the pictures of his finishing run in the T. M. Ahern Memorial Handicap and without expecting ever to see an actual horse achieve such a victory.

I found so much meaning in Bernborough finishes that I looked for them in fields other than horse racing, although with little success. At the Bendigo Thousand professional athletics meeting each year, I watched the tailenders in the last lap of every long-distance race, willing them to sweep around the field and to gather in the leaders. I sometimes persuaded my brother and a few of the children from next door to take part in a race of several laps around our house. Early in each race, I dropped far behind the second-last runner. In the language of racing commentators, I was going to come from nowhere or from the clouds; I was going to descend on the leaders or to drop on them in the shadows of the post or to do a Bernborough; but I was mostly an also-ran.

Of all the Melbourne Cups that I've watched, I recall most often that of 1983 when Kiwi (Dark blue, white crossed sashes, red armbands, pale-blue cap) trailed the field into the straight and won running away. The Oakleigh Plate is a sprint of 1100 metres, and yet I've been twice fortunate to see the winner come from last at the top of the comparatively short Caulfield straight. New Statesman (Blue, red striped sleeves, yellow cap) did it in 1962 and Woorim (Black-and-white quarters, orange cap) in 2012.

Perhaps I was trying to arrange a Bernborough performance for myself in 1957. I had passed the matriculation exam with honours in every subject but, rather than go to university as all my friends did, I hid myself for three months in a Catholic seminary, then worked as a junior clerk, and then enrolled in a two-year course at a teachers' college. I buried myself in the ruck of primary teachers for the next ten years and used all my spare time to write a work of fiction of nearly two hundred thousand words with horse racing as one of its major themes and a section with the title 'Bernborough comes down from the north'.

4. *We Backed Money Moon*

PLENTY ROAD IN Bundoora comprises nowadays six lanes of motor traffic and two tram tracks, but in the early 1940s it was a narrow bitumen road leading through open countryside north of Melbourne. A medical centre of several storeys stands today on the north-east corner of the intersection of Plenty Road and Kingsbury Drive, and nearby is one of the entrances to the vast campus of La Trobe University, but in the early 1940s Kingsbury Drive did not exist and on the site of the medical centre and the university car park were farm buildings and workers' cottages. My parents and my two brothers and I lived in one of those cottages during my third and fourth and fifth years, and I have numerous memories from that time. One memory is of my mother's calling me, on a certain warm afternoon, to the wireless set, as we called it, and telling me to hope that the horse Dark Felt would win the Melbourne Cup, which was about to be run. Dark Felt (Pink, black bands and cap) duly won the Melbourne Cup of 1943, and my father bought from his winnings the first motorcar that I recall having travelled in.

My father was assistant manager of the farm attached to several mental hospitals, as they were then called. Larundel, Mont Park, and Macleod hospitals were known to me only as huge buildings in the distance, but some of the trusted inmates—shabbily dressed old men who muttered to themselves—sometimes brought milk to our door or did odd jobs around our house and garden. Our house was one of a long row of such houses stretching north from near the Preston Cemetery to somewhere out of my view. The houses faced westwards, towards a rudimentary golf course on the other side of Plenty Road where the suburb of Kingsbury now stands. The leading male occupant of each house worked on the farm or in the hospitals. The men were employees of the state government and their pay would have been modest, but their being provided with low-rental houses would have helped them to live comfortably. I can call to mind a few names: Joe Hall the electrician, Percy Pinches the carpenter—a hard name to forget!—Dave Speedie, whose occupation I've forgotten, and George Kelly who was, I think, a gardener. I cannot recall the appearance of the first three but George I remember well, probably because he lived next door to us.

George and Bernadette Kelly were a childless couple then aged, perhaps, in their late forties. George was lean and leathery, with a face I recall as suntanned, although his having died only a few years later makes me wonder today whether he might have been permanently flushed from drinking. Bernadette was taller than George, thin, dark of hair and complexion and, according to a set of standards that I had devised even as a small boy, good-looking. She was the first woman that I recall seeing in make-up and smoking cigarettes. I surely saw Bernadette often, given that she lived next door, but now, as I write, my only clear memories of her derive from the one Sunday morning that I'm about to report. Did my mother avoid Bernadette? Or, more likely, did my father discourage my mother from mixing with a woman who smoked and drank and wore make-up?

I recall from my three years at Bundoora only two Sunday mornings. On one of the two, my father and I spent a half-hour or more with George and Bernadette Kelly in their lounge room. On the other Sunday morning, my father and I attended mass in the Church of the Sacred Heart in Preston. My parents were good Catholics, to use an expression of those times, and would never have missed Sunday mass for any light reason. Our house on the hospitals' farmland, however, was six kilometres from the nearest church, which would have excused us from attending mass if we had had no other means of getting to church than by walking, which was mostly our situation. A Catholic family from the neighbourhood, whose name I've forgotten, sometimes found a place for two of our family in their large motorcar. I have no recollection of the family or of travelling in their car to and from Bell Street, Preston, but I seem to have gone there to mass sometimes with my father while the older of my brothers went sometimes with my mother. My only memory of any sort of religious observance during my years at Bundoora is as follows.

The morning is warm and sunny, and the side doors of the church have been left open. From my seat beside my father, I can see across Bell Street into the front gardens of several single-fronted cottages. Bell Street has long since become a six-lane major road, but passing cars are so few in the early 1940s that I am able to hear from my seat just inside the church the whirring of a hand mower pushed by a bald man in his shirtsleeves backwards and forwards across a tiny patch of buffalo grass in front of one of the houses opposite. The man and his mowing must have attracted me more than the ceremonies in the church; I recall my father's elbow several times digging into my side and his finger pointing me back towards the altar.

On the other of my two remembered Sundays, I am seated in a comfortable armchair while my father and the Kelly couple, all three of them seated and at ease, discuss the race meeting of the previous day, which would have been at Flemington or Moonee Valley or Mentone, given that the courses at Caulfield and Williamstown served as army camps throughout the Second World War. All three adults in the room attended the race meeting, wherever it was. My father would have gone alone, as always. George and Bernadette Kelly, like thousands of other working-class couples in that era, would have dressed in their best clothes, he in a suit and tie and she in a coat and hat, and would have considered the outing their chief social event for the week. In the trams and trains that they travelled on, most of the passengers would have been racegoers or, if the season was winter, a mixture of racegoers and football followers, and the Kellys and their like would often, on their homeward journey, have had with strangers the sort of conversation that they had with my father on the Sunday in question.

I cannot account for my father's and my being where we were on that morning. My father never visited anyone for merely social purposes, and I don't recall his being especially friendly towards George Kelly, who would have seemed to my father no more than a mug punter obliged to read form guides for lack of the inside information that my father was able to obtain. Anyway, there we were, and I've remembered for more than seventy years what was almost certainly my only visit to that lounge room.

While I loll on floral-patterned velvet upholstery, I take more interest in what I can see around me than what I can hear. The floor of the room is covered, most of it, by a carpet square, something that I have never previously seen. The space between the perimeter of the carpet and the skirting board has been stained the same colour as the soft drink that I am sipping. When Mrs Kelly served me the drink, she told me it was sarsaparilla. The word is new to me, and I try to persuade myself that the flavour of the stuff in my glass is as strange and exotic as its name. Each of the other three persons in the room has a drink in hand, and each drink is a different shade of golden brown, as though all four of us have been served according to a scale of colour, with me being the possessor of the richest gradation. (Not that it matters, but I decided just now that Bernadette would have been drinking beer and George whisky, while my father had some sort of ginger-coloured soft drink.) George and Bernadette smoke cigarettes continually. George rolls his from a yellow and red tin of tobacco, while Bernadette draws hers out with her fingertips from a packet showing the silhouettes in black and white of an elegantly groomed man and woman. Standing on the carpet halfway between George and Bernadette is the item of furniture that tells me more eloquently than anything else in the room that the Kellys are more privileged than my own family. Was it called a smokers' stand? It was made of stainless steel and some early variety of plastic. It had a circular base and an ornamental top and, halfway between, ashtrays and fixtures for holding packets of cigarettes. George annoys me by flicking his ash carelessly into the tray nearer him, but Bernadette wins me over with her way of uncrossing her legs and then leaning forward and tap-tap-tapping the end of her cigarette with her index finger. This she does time and again, and I never fail to watch her every movement.

The three adults discussed one after another of the races on the previous day's program. Being still too young to understand the business of betting, I failed to follow much of the conversation. If my mother had happened to ask me afterwards for details, I could not have obliged her. And yet, I've remembered for more than seventy years a short statement made by Bernadette Kelly on that long-ago Sunday morning and have remembered also some of what I felt on hearing the statement.

A certain race and its winner had been mentioned for the first time, probably by my father. Before anything else could be said, Bernadette Kelly delivered the sentence that gives this section its title, and I like to think that she delivered it while tapping her cigarette ash into one of the trays on the smokers' stand that I so admired. Her emphasis was on the first of the four words, as though to tell my father and, perhaps, myself that he or we would have been foolish to surmise that two punters as shrewd and successful as she and George could have wavered for an instant in their determination to back such a certainty as Money Moon (colours unknown). If she said more than this, I never afterwards recalled it and probably failed to hear it while I leaned back against the headrest of my chair and sipped my sarsaparilla and began to assemble the details of a daydream scene in which the words *money* and *moon* denoted much more than a successful racehorse.

Just above the horizon of a faraway picture-book landscape of fields and hills and woodlands and spires in distant villages, a huge orange-gold moon is rising. The moon has the same rich colour as the liquids in the glasses of the inhabitants of the landscape: fortunate folk who sit at leisure in their lounge rooms. Or the moon has the same colour as the tobacco in the cigarettes that the fortunate ones lift to their lips or tap into their elaborate ashtrays. This is the landscape not only of Money Moon but of Honeymoon, for I have heard that word already and am able faintly to conjecture what a man might feel on being alone with his good-looking dark-haired wife in a richly lit landscape. The landscape of my vision is remote from me, and not just because of my being still a child. Before I can hope to enter the territory of Money/Honeymoon, I must devote myself to learning the immensely complicated lore of horse racing.

I lived for about three years in Bundoora. Let's say, in round figures, that I spent a hundred and fifty Sunday mornings there. Let's suppose further that my father and I attended mass in Preston every six weeks, having been taken there by the family that I've wholly forgotten. That amounts to twenty-five masses in the Church of the Sacred Heart. But my father surely drove us all to mass every Sunday during the few months while he owned the Nash sedan that

33

was paid for by Dark Felt. (He owned the splendid car only briefly before having to sell it during a run of losing bets.) So, in round figures again, I attended forty masses while living in Bundoora. Of the forty hours that I spent in church I recall only the few minutes while I watched the man mowing his lawn. I recall no sight of altar or vestments, no tinkling of bells, no word or gesture from the pulpit. Perhaps I visited the Kelly lounge room on more than one Sunday morning, although I suspect not. The question, however, is irrelevant. On the scoreboard of memories from my Sundays in Bundoora, the Kelly lounge room has easily defeated the Church of the Sacred Heart.

During the fifteen years after I left Bundoora, I attended mass faithfully every Sunday and was much affected by my Catholic beliefs. On a few brief occasions, I experienced a sort of religious fervour, and for six months in my eighteenth year I even supposed I was called to be a priest. My writing this account of my Sunday morning with boozy George Kelly and chain-smoking, dark-haired Bernadette has convinced me, though, that my religious faith rested on foundations that were flimsy indeed by comparison with my faith in—what should I call it?—the dream-world brought into being by the sight of richly tinted drinks and the sound of mellifluous horse names.

5. *Gerald and Geraldo*

I WAS NAMED after a racehorse. I knew this from an early age and considered it a distinction. I asked my father few questions about the equine Gerald. However, I learned from one of my father's brothers after my father had died that my namesake had shown much promise when young but was later such a disappointment that he was sold by his owners. (When my father died in my twenty-first year he was certainly disappointed in me, although he had not gone so far as to disown me.)

My father's name may well have appeared in race books as the owner or part-owner of Gerald (Black, blue sleeves, red band and cap) when he raced in and around Melbourne in the late 1930s. My father was certainly registered as the owner and the trainer of Geraldo (Yellow, black cap), which won a race at Kyneton and another at Cranbourne in 1950 but was later, like Gerald, sold at auction. And yet, my father would have paid not a penny towards the purchase price or the upkeep of either horse—he was a front man or a dummy for a man he sometimes called his best friend but who might be said to have been his evil genius. This was a man named Edwin Ettershank, known always as Teddy. I had him in mind while I wrote about the character Lenny Goodchild in *Tamarisk Row*, my first published book. The boy Clement, the chief character of *Tamarisk Row*, has never met Lenny and thinks of him as a mysterious racing mastermind in faraway Melbourne. I met Teddy Ettershank a number of times but never knew what to make of him.

I'll write more about Teddy in due course. Just now, I want to write about another matter altogether. For most of my life, I've railed in vain against an absurd practice followed by race stewards when upholding a protest by connections of a horse finishing third against a horse finishing first. Such a protest is lodged when the first horse past the post has interfered so severely with a rival that the rival finishes not even second but third, having been passed near the post by an innocent bystander, so to speak—a horse not at all involved in the bumping or the crossing of paths. For as long as I can recall, the stewards, if they deem that interference prevented the victim from finishing ahead of the interferer, then go on to award first place to the innocent bystander, as I called the second place-getter. Presumably, the stewards are punishing the interfering horse by placing it behind the victim of the interference. And yet, this goes against common sense. The interfering horse beat the innocent bystander on its merits. If no interference had taken place, then the third horse past the post would have finished first and the innocent bystander would have finished third. This is the situation that the stewards should aim to restore. To put the matter another way: instead of punishing the interferer, the stewards should compensate the victim of interference by putting it ahead of the horse that cost it the race.

All of the above seems blindingly obvious to me, but every few years I seethe with anger and frustration when a protest by a third placegetter is upheld and the second placegetter is awarded the race. Then I seethe even more when I hear some know-all journalist or even one of the stewards trying to explain the crazy decision. The more they talk, the more confused they become. One of their favourite arguments is that the second placegetter must not be punished unjustly. Fair enough, but neither should the second placegetter be *rewarded* unjustly. Never, under any circumstances, was the second placegetter—the innocent bystander, as I have called it—going to win. If the race had been run without interference, the innocent one would have finished *third*, and the victim of interference would have won. I can't put it more simply than that, and yet the so-called experts have been getting it wrong during my seventy years as a follower of racing and probably for much longer.

Luckily, the stupidity that I'm complaining about prevails only once or twice every decade in Victoria. After one instance, about twenty years ago, I wrote a short letter to the editor of the weekly *Winning Post*. The letter was published, and for a few days I hoped that my few simple paragraphs would be read by someone of influence who would talk to someone else of even more influence, and so on, until an ancient wrong would be righted at last. Nothing of the sort happened. I thought at least one other reader might have written to the editor in support of my argument, but no such letter was published.

Perhaps ten years ago, after another of the monstrous injustices had been perpetrated, I found among the letters to the editor of *Winning Post* a letter rather like my earlier one. The writer was Bruno Cannatelli, a well-known photographer who attends every Melbourne race meeting. I had never spoken to Bruno but I did so a few weeks later at Sandown. I felt encouraged to be speaking to someone who shared my own views, but I wondered how we two could ever convince the thick-headed majority.

After I wrote that paragraph above about Teddy Ettershank, I left off writing for a few days. I travelled to Melbourne to see the Caulfield Cup. (I'm writing these pages in 2013, and the Cup was won by Fawkner, carrying Dark blue, white armbands and cap.) On the day before the Cup, I attended the annual dinner of the Thoroughbred Club of Australia. Along with ten others on my table, I was a guest of Kevin O'Brien. Kevin and his wife, Tanith, are proprietors of Lauriston Stud at Corinella (Orange and green quarters and quartered cap). Near me at the table was Bruno Cannatelli. I reminded him that we had met a few years before at Sandown and had shared our views on protests. I told him that I had since left Melbourne and hardly ever mixed with racing folk any more, whereas he was a widely known and well-respected racegoer. I urged him to go on fighting the good fight: to try to persuade anyone who would listen that a better way exists for the settling of protests by third placegetters against winners.

I may have sounded to Bruno as though I had given up the cause, but I'll make this one last effort. I hereby appeal to all fair-minded readers of these pages. Surely you can appreciate the injustice of the present system of amending the placings after a successful protest by the third placegetter against the first horse past the post. And surely, also, you can appreciate the fairness of my suggestion for changing the present system. Well then, fair-minded reader, would you please talk to other racegoers about these matters? Would you use whatever influence you might have to bring forward the day when the stewards use common sense and not quaint rules of their own whenever they amend the placings after a certain sort of protest?

Fawkner's Caulfield Cup is only a memory now, and I'm back at my desk trying to describe Teddy Ettershank. He was small enough to have been a jockey or, at least, a track rider. He must have applied, at some time, for a licence to train; my father told me once that the then chief steward, Alan Bell, had said to Teddy, the hopeful applicant, 'As long as I'm chairman of the VRC stewards, Ettershank, you'll never be a licensed trainer.' Nowadays, a person in Teddy's position would seek legal advice and would exercise his right of appeal to this and that higher authority. In Teddy's heyday and mine, the issuing or the withdrawal of licences was wholly the province of the stewards. All their hearings and enquiries were carried out behind closed doors. An aggrieved person could appeal against the stewards' decision but only to the committee of the Victoria Racing Club, the employers of the stewards. (I am not at all implying that racing was less ably managed then than now. In fact, I incline to the opposite view.) Anyway, Teddy was never a licensed trainer or even a registered owner, although he certainly owned and trained many a horse, using my father and others as front men or dummies, and I suspect that he enjoyed his reputation as a man of mystery. In Teddy's time racing, as I've explained by now, was much concerned with secret knowledge, and Teddy was widely believed to have an abundance of such knowledge. I never saw him followed by a knot of spectators, as Jim Jenkins and other noted punters were sometimes followed, but if Teddy and his trusted man, Gerald Lavers (another Gerald!), had backed a horse, news of their doing so was soon all through the betting ring.

What seems most remarkable about Teddy as I recall him today, three or four decades after his death, is that he was never observed to engage in any sort of paid employment. Put plainly, he never had a job, a position, a calling. My father said sometimes that Teddy lived by his wits. I wonder how Teddy described his occupation on his taxation returns, assuming that he bothered to submit them. The expression *professional punter* was not much used in the years when Teddy was most active. Persons describing themselves thus in recent decades have mostly turned out to be launderers of money gained from other sources. No such suspicion was ever attached to Teddy. In the absence of any evidence to the contrary, I'm obliged to report that Teddy Ettershank was the only man I ever met who supported himself wholly by betting on racehorses.

When I first heard of Teddy, he was a widower and aged probably in his forties. He owned a comfortable house in the Travancore estate, in what was then the better part of Ascot Vale and not far from Flemington racecourse. He lived with his mother and Gerald, his only child. Teddy always drove a near-new car. He sent his son to Melbourne Grammar and later to university. When Teddy was in his fifties, so I heard afterwards, he married a much younger woman and became the father of at least two more children. To the best of my knowledge, he financed all this from the proceeds of his betting.

My father, as I wrote earlier, called Teddy his best friend, but even as a boy I saw that the two men were not equals: my father was more like a client or even a hanger-on. My father visited Teddy often and phoned him even more often. I can't recall my father's receiving any phone calls from Teddy, and I suspect that Teddy's one visit to our house, in 1950, when we lived in Pascoe Vale, was for the purpose of taking my father in haste to Geraldo's stable, there to pose as the horse's true owner and so to avert some possible crisis with officialdom. Teddy's information certainly helped my father to collect some lucrative bets. On the evening of Geraldo's win at Cranbourne, I saw my father counting out a share of his winnings to my mother in their bedroom—the bedspread was covered with brick-red ten-pound notes, each of them worth much more than five hundred dollars today. In 1956, after my father had had to sell our house to pay his gambling debts, he won the deposit on another house by backing one of Teddy's tips in a race at Mornington. (The horse was named Valley Vista—Pale-green and purple hoops—and had poor form, and yet it won easily at short odds, causing my father to suspect, and to whisper to me under pain of secrecy, that Teddy had organised, or had at least been privy to, an old-fashioned ring-in.) It may well be true, and my father sometimes ruefully postulated it, that if he had never followed his own opinions when betting but had backed only Teddy's recommended horses, he would have had a successful career as a punter, but this is to suggest that Teddy was more open and more benevolent than he actually was.

Towards the end of *Tamarisk Row*, Augustine Killeaton has one last, desperate bet and loses. As a result, he has to flee from the city of Bassett and the bookmakers that he has no hope of paying. He makes his ruinous bet after receiving some incomplete information from the man that he calls the Master, Lenny Goodchild, in faraway Melbourne. Augustine is too ashamed to contact Goodchild afterwards, and the next week the horse that ruined him lands a massive plunge, as a racing writer would put it. Augustine is more distressed to have been left out of Goodchild's operation than to have missed out on winning enough to settle his debts. Nothing so dramatic ever happened between my father and Teddy. I even recall Teddy's visiting my father in hospital on the day before he died unexpectedly. And yet I had in mind while I invented my fictional goings-on a few occasions when my father seemed on the point of admitting that Teddy sometimes kept from him things that my father deserved to be told and one occasion when my father was telling me about the disappointing career of my namesake in the years before my birth. He recalled a day when Gerald had run unplaced at Moonee Valley. My father had backed the horse heavily and he wondered aloud in my hearing whether Teddy had arranged that day to have the horse beaten and had absentmindedly, or even deliberately, not told my father.

I called this section after two horses linked to me by name. When I planned the section, I intended to end it with the information that both horses, Gerald and Geraldo, were sold in mid-career and afterwards did surprisingly well for their new owners and trainers. Gerald won a number of races in Western Australia and Geraldo in the Wangaratta district of Victoria. I was going to speculate that

I was somewhat like my horsey namesakes, in that I performed better after having got away from the influence of my father. Even his early death played into my hands. How could I have written *Tamarisk Row* while he was still alive?

Yes, I named this section after two horses, but it was taken over, you might say, by the man who secretly owned the horses and had such a powerful influence on my father. I don't think often nowadays about my father but, whenever I do, I think also about Teddy Ettershank, who could probably be said to have been my father's hero. Or, rather, I think about a man named Ettershank who might be Teddy himself but is more likely Teddy's father or even grandfather. My father once told me that Teddy's forebears had been racing men from around Flemington for several generations. Ettershank, the image-man in my mind, always appears to me as though he stands in close conversation with another image-man on the day in September when the first north wind blows from the inland across Melbourne and then across the bay and out into Bass Strait. The connotations are obvious to me. Spring and early warm weather in Melbourne are linked with the Spring Racing Carnival, perhaps the greatest racing carnival in the world, as European trainers and owners have only recently learned to their surprise, and the first north wind reminds persons such as myself that another Spring Carnival is in the offing.

Little survives today of what I call Old Flemington but, as recently as thirty years ago, I could drive from Epsom Road along Sandown Road towards Ascot Vale Road on my way home from a meeting at Flemington racecourse and could call to mind easily how the area must have been during the Great Age of Racing, which began eighty years before my birth and ended twenty years after it. Nearly every house in Sandown Road had behind it a paved stable yard and half a dozen loose boxes with a feed loft above them. In the decades when motorcars were rarities, the streets in the early morning darkness echoed with the clatter of horseshoes on bitumen as hundreds of horses walked from their stables in streets all around to be exercised at Flemington racecourse. Generations of Ettershanks would have been up and active before dawn, but my defining scene takes place in early afternoon during the few hours when racing men (they were always men in those days) had some brief, precious leisure time before the horses in their care required their afternoon exercise. My defining scene takes place against a background of pepper trees, probably because the old Newmarket sale yards were lined with such trees and a few still stand in the now-fashionable quarter of Kensington that was established after the closure of the yards. The warm north wind agitates the dense green foliage of the pepper trees in some shabby street near Flemington racecourse, and the same wind overlays all of my defining scene with a golden mist.

We think of air pollution as something relatively new, but a woman of my mother's age told me once that when she worked as a young shop assistant in Melbourne in the 1930s the streets of the city were always spattered with horse dung. In cold or rainy weather, the stuff lay moist where it had fallen. In hot weather, it soon dried, and when the north wind blew in spring and summer the air above the streets was thick with particles of yellow chaff flung up from the desiccated dung. The same yellow haze swirls around my mythical Ettershank and his nameless companion while they stand beneath the waving pepper trees somewhere in Old Flemington on a spring afternoon long before my birth and while they devise together a plot against the bookmakers. I hear nothing of what passes between mythical-Ettershank and his mate but I hear a paraphrase of a passage I last read as a schoolboy. I hear Macbeth's declaring that terrible things were done in the olden time.

The previous paragraph might well have been a suitable ending for this section, but I can end it perhaps even more aptly by reporting my sister's reaction when she first met Teddy Ettershank. She was not quite one year of age and was perched in her mother's arms when the diminutive egg-bald man strode into our kitchen in Pascoe Vale, stepped up close to her, and made what he surely intended to be a friendly noise. My sister turned her face to her mother's shoulder and burst into tears.

6. A. R. Sands, Demigod

RACE MEETINGS OF fifty and more years ago attracted huge crowds by comparison with today, and yet the facilities in the public areas, as distinct from the members' areas, would be considered intolerable nowadays. My father and I travelled by train to the Derby Day meeting at Flemington in November 1956. We stood and swayed among the press of passengers in one of the dozens of special race trains running express from Spencer Street Station to the platform beside the racecourse. The weather was fine and warm, and the betting ring and its surrounds were densely crowded all day, except for the few minutes when a race was being run. Surely there were seats provided somewhere but, as I recall it, my father and I spent most of the day standing in the ring or edging our way with thousands of others to and from the lawn before and after each race. This was in the public enclosure, as it was called. We understood that things were different in the members' enclosure. We glimpsed some of the members on the far side of the so-called rails, where leading bookmakers took bets from both us, the paying public, and them, the members of the Victoria Racing Club, all of them men and many wearing the top hats and morning dress that was traditional on Derby Day. The members' enclosure was shaded by elm trees, with plentiful seating beneath, and overhung by the massive members' grandstand, with spacious dining rooms and bars on its ground floor. We tens of thousands who had paid the equivalent of about seventy-five dollars in today's currency had only a small grandstand that was full long before each race. My father was one of the many who liked to stay in the ring until the late money arrived, and so we watched each race from the lawn, which was not even sloped or elevated and from which most spectators saw nothing of the horses until they rushed past in the straight. The weather on Derby Day in 1956, as I've reported, was fine and warm. If rain had fallen, a few of us might have found shelter in the public bars or in the lee of the totalisator building, but the rest of us could have done no more than turn our backs to the weather like sheep or cattle.

My father never read a form guide or a race book. He learned all that he needed to know by watching the betting or listening to smart men, as he called them. His philosophy of racing, so to call it, had been developed on a single afternoon at the Warrnambool racecourse, which is about halfway between his birthplace at Allansford and his grave in the Warrnambool Cemetery, beside the estuary of the Hopkins River.

Reginald Thomas Murnane died in his fifties more than fifty years ago, and I often wish I had questioned him more about his racing exploits while I had the opportunity. He was a talkative man and he would willingly have told me about plunges planned months in advance, secret track gallops, certainties beaten by the narrowest of margins, or bookmakers asking for time to pay up, but I recall only brief anecdotes and off-hand references.

How old was he when he went to the Warrnambool races for the first time? I estimate the date to have been in the early 1920s, when he was about twenty. He was the eldest son of a prosperous dairy farmer and might have become a farmer himself, but his life changed when his appendix burst at the age of sixteen. His family expected him to die, yet he survived thanks to a remarkable medico at the Warrnambool Hospital, a man named Bannon, who spent hours cleaning out of my father's guts every last skerrick of the muck that might have led to fatal septicaemia if it had remained inside him after his surgical procedure. My father spent a year recuperating, and during that time he visited cousins in New South Wales and Queensland, and developed his lifelong love of travel and changes of scenery. Perhaps he went to his first race meetings during that time, when he was far away from his father, whom I remember from my childhood as the unsmiling tyrant of the household. All I learned from my father are a few details of the fateful Warrnambool meeting mentioned already.

My father would have known numerous locals at the Warrnambool races, but the famous steeplechase meeting in May drew owners and trainers and punters and bookmakers from Melbourne and elsewhere. These would have been unknown to my father, and yet, early during the meeting he identified a group who knew what they were about. Or, did he identify more than one such group? He stood unobtrusively near them. He followed them. He backed what they backed. He won money, and more money, and here I must digress.

Whether it was the result of that first wondrous day at Warrnambool races or whether it came from some natural reckless-ness in him, my father could never bet responsibly, to use that sanctimonious expression. He handed over to my mother every fortnight the modest salary cheque that he earned as a low-level public servant, and he lived frugally, neither drinking nor smoking. When he bet, however, he seemed to forget the monetary scale that governed his everyday affairs. He seemed to think he was an owner or a trainer or one of his revered smart men. If someone he respected tipped him a horse, my father would bet on it, at the very least, a sum equal to half his weekly earnings. If he did not have such a sum at hand, he usually knew an illegal off-course bookmaker who would let him bet on credit. In his bachelor years (he did not marry until he was thirty-four), he won many a time a sum that might have bought a block of land in an outer suburb or even a single-fronted cottage in a working-class inner suburb. And yet, his and my mother's first home after their marriage was a room with a double bed in a board-ing house in Brunswick. He wore a bespoke suit and a gold-plated Rolex Prince watch and one or another of a collection of grey felt hats with peacock feathers in their bands, but he died with no assets to speak of and owing many thousands of dollars in today's currency to his brothers and to who knows how many bookmakers that he welshed on, to put it bluntly.

The first race on Derby Day in 1956 was the Wakeful Stakes for three-years-old fillies. It was contested by better-than-average fillies being prepared, most of them, for the Oaks Stakes on the following Thursday. The favourite, at very short odds, was In Harmony (Green and yellow hoops), trained locally by Stan Murphy. My father and I had only just arrived in the betting ring when he grabbed my elbow and hissed at me to follow a certain man who had just brushed past us and to learn which horse the man was going to back with the several ten-pound notes that he held in his hand. If the reader wonders why my father himself did not follow the man, then the reader has still not understood my attempts to describe how it was in the Great Age of Racing, which had begun nearly a century before the day when my father told me to spy on Alf Sands and which, had we only known it, was about to end within the next decade. My father was vain and had an inflated sense of his own place in the world, but at the races he truly did have the appearance of a smart man, of someone *in the know*. Even I, still a schoolboy, knew that if my father had followed Alf Sands, then Alf, being at least as smart as my father, would have got wind of it and would have put his money into his pocket and lost himself in the crowd.

And so, I followed Alf, as I'll call him hence, to the rear of the ring, where I observed him put his thirty pounds, win-only, on a filly named Sandara (Red, black spots) at the odds of thirty-three-to-one. In fact, the bookmaker, following accepted custom, rounded off the bet. Alf stood to win a thousand pounds for his thirty pounds. I estimate the value of the outlay in today's currency to have been at least fifteen hundred dollars and the value of the winnings, if the bet succeeded, to have been at least fifty thousand, and I still marvel at how bets of that size were considered modest indeed in 1956 and could be placed with no fuss with any of the lesser bookmakers at the rear of the ring.

I reported Alf's bet to my father, and we consulted the race book in order to learn what possible connection existed between the outsider Sandara, which was trained at Flemington by a man named Burke, and Alf, who managed his stables at far-off Epsom, in Mordialloc. The connection was not hard to find. Sandara was to be ridden by Alan Yeomans, a leading jockey who had been (he may have been still—I don't remember) apprenticed to Alf. Now, in those days, the Code of Racing, so to call it, had as its first command-ment 'Thou shalt not take the Stable's market.' The commandment acknowledged that the owner and trainer and stable followers of a horse with a good winning chance had first entitlement to the best of the odds bet about the horse. Any outsider happening to know of the horse's ability and daring to alert the bookmakers with an early rush of money would reduce the odds available to the stable and would thereby commit racing's worst crime. Sometimes a jockey would be in a position to commit this crime. He might be engaged to ride the horse although he was a freelance unconnected with the stable. In all my years as a follower of racing, I heard of only three instances of a jockey's getting his own money on at top odds, being found out, and being afterwards punished. (Jockeys, of course, are prohibited from betting but who can police their betting through proxies?) Their punishment was severe indeed. Word of their crime was soon all over Melbourne, if not Victoria; their telephones stopped ringing; their careers were as good as over. My father and I understood at once why Alf was backing Sandara and why he was doing it on the outer edges of the ring. The jockey had passed on certain information to Alf, who could act on it but only with the utmost discretion. Alan Yeomans took Sandara to the lead soon after the start, and the filly was never in danger of being beaten. My father won a hundred pounds on the race with an outlay of only three.

I can report little else about the actual Alf Sands but much about the figure of that name who was one of the demigods in my private mythology of racing. I recall the afternoon when my father made a special trip to Caulfield after having heard from someone he trusted that the Sands stable was going to back one of several horses of theirs engaged that day. My father had no trouble identifying the horse when the time came. Pageoptic (some or another combination of yellow, green, and purple) had been performing only moderately for months past on provincial tracks, but was backed from sixteen-to-one into ten-to-one and won handsomely, and my father arrived home with his pockets bulging—metaphorically, if not literally.

One day in 1958, I read a newspaper report of a successful plunge at Werribee on a Sands-trained horse named Beau Conde (some or another combination of purple, yellow, and red). After the race, a woman had collected the winnings. She had gone from bookmaker to bookmaker, putting rolls of banknotes into a briefcase.

I have reported only three of Alf Sands' many achievements, but these should be enough for my purposes. I have believed for most of my life in my private legend of Alf Sands, by which I mean that I have believed in a mythical man able to prevail against the odds. Sometimes his stable commissioners stride past one after another rails bookmaker, challenging each to risk the most he dares on a horse at long odds and with moderate form. At other times, the man himself lurks at the rear of the betting ring, looking to profit modestly from information obtained in the utmost secrecy. This man may have the appearance of the man that my father pointed out to me at Flemington in 1956, but much about him is other than factual. And so, A. R. Sands the demigod, as I call him, may have the sandy hair and the alert expression of the man that I followed through the betting ring, but whereas the man who backed Sandara had a wife and at least one child, my hero is unencumbered by domestic concerns. In his private life he resembles Jack Holt, a renowned trainer of the 1920s and 1930s, who became known as the Wizard of Mordialloc on account of his many successful betting coups. (It was a coincidence that both my hero-trainers had their stables at the same racecourse.) Holt was a lifelong bachelor who lived simply with his two unmarried sisters as housekeepers and companions. He had been born into poverty but amassed a fortune, most of which he bequeathed to charity.

Worshipping a demigod is rather like being in love—not the sort of love depicted in films or described in romance novels but the irrational, obsessive passion that has sometimes taken hold of me and that caused me to think for many years that I was unique, until I learned otherwise from reading the fiction of Marcel Proust. The worshipper of a demigod, far from approaching the object of worship, hangs back, keeps at a distance, remains for the time being unknown. For months, or even for years, it is enough for the worshipper to know that the demigod exists and is available for observation. During this period of preparation, the worshipper has to learn all that can possibly be learned about the demigod's whims, preferences, beliefs, whatever comes under the heading of *way of life*. At the same time, the worshipper has to change, to improve, and to become worthy of the notice of the demigod at some fortunate time in the far future. Perhaps I exaggerate, but I can recall myself in late 1957 and early 1958 noting the details of every race start of every horse trained by Alf Sands. I had set myself the impossible task of learning from a longitudinal study of his horses' careers how to predict when he was about to launch a betting plunge on one or another of them.

I recall a day in 1958 when I absented myself from the teachers' college that I was obliged to attend daily. I travelled by bus to the Redan racecourse (Ballarat had two racecourses in those days—Dowling Forest and Redan). I was confident that one of the two Sands horses engaged that day would be well backed and would win. I even had the vague and absurd hope that one of the trusted stable punters, or even Alf himself, might see me collecting my modest winnings after the race and might be so impressed by my sagacity as to make himself known to me. (From this may be learned one of the several great differences between myself and my father, who were driven in opposite directions by our obsession with racing. He bet boldly and thrust himself into the company of the insiders, the smart men that he so admired; I bet timidly and dreamed about my admired characters from afar.) Nothing of the sort happened, and Alf's horses finished well back after having drifted in the betting.

At the height of my infatuation with A. R. Sands and his ways, I noted that he had an entrant in the Melbourne Cup. This was in 1957, when I worked for a few months as a junior clerk, filling in time before I could begin my course at a primary teachers' college. The man at the next desk was named Martin Dillon. He will be mentioned in another section of this book. He too was a racing tragic, although the expression had not yet been devised at that time. He had a great respect for Alf Sands but I could not persuade him that Alf's horse was in the Cup with a genuine chance, as a racing journalist might have put it. Mr Dillon, as I called him (he was white-haired and sixtyish; I was eighteen) tried to explain to me that most owners of racehorses would be proud to have a horse good enough merely to compete in the Melbourne Cup and that the owners of Alf's horse were surely no exception. The horse was named Carbea (its colours will be mentioned below); it had been running unplaced in recent country events; and its odds were a hundred-to-one. I did not claim that Carbea could win but I had convinced myself that it must have been much better than its form suggested if Alf Sands had approved of its being entered in the Cup. I bet Mr Dillon a pound (one-eighth of my weekly wage) that Carbea would finish in the first third of the field. In racing parlance, Carbea never flattered at any stage. He finished seventeenth of nineteen, and Mr Dillon said he had never earned a pound more easily.

Something else that Marcel Proust, forty and more years before my birth, discovered about lover-worshippers: they change their own likes and preferences to match those of their idols. I had been evaluating racing colours for some years before I became a devotee of Alf Sands. At no time had the colours gold and red appealed to me until I learned that the colours of the Sands stable were Gold, red stars and cuffs. It required some effort of the imagination (I would have preferred my hero's coat of arms to have been more muted and subtle), but I came to approve of the rich gold and the fiery red as denoters of accumulating wealth and a defiance of convention. I even found an admirable contrariness in the fact that the *background* was gold and not the stars themselves, as might have been expected.

Another fact about Alf that I accommodated after some early difficulty was his connection with the city of Grafton, in northern New South Wales. As a boy, I had settled on what would be my ideal landscapes for the rest of my life: the green and mostly level countryside of south-western Victoria. Even then, I had developed what would become a lifelong dislike of travel. If, for some reason, I had been obliged to leave the state of Victoria, I might have endured a move to Tasmania or New Zealand but to nowhere else. Queensland, and even New South Wales, seemed subtropical and alien places, but I learned by some or another means that Alf Sands and his family often spent the winter in Grafton, taking a few horses with them and racing them locally. Perhaps I was helped to accept this by my learning that jacaranda trees abound in Grafton. At that time, I supposed that my own racing colours ought to be partly lilac or lavender or mauve. Perhaps the jacarandas of Grafton were not even in bloom during Alf's sojourn there, but I saw him often as walking his horses of a morning or afternoon through an intermittent shower of blossoms of one of my favourite colours, and I forgave him any bafflement he might have caused me by his travelling northwards.

From the 1960s onwards, the career of the actual A. R. Sands might be said to have levelled out or even declined. Heavily backed horses might be comfortably beaten into second or third place when, in earlier years, they would either win or be narrowly beaten. My father, who was no longer alive to witness the gradual decline of the man he had once called the smartest trainer in Melbourne—my father might have said that the elderly Alf had lost his touch, but I supposed that my hero was no longer driven as in earlier years. Like Jack Holt, he would have invested much of his winnings in real estate and shares; he no longer depended on racing for his livelihood.

When last I saw his name in print, A. R. Sands was training an occasional winner in Brisbane, which is a place I have never felt the least inclination to visit. I assume that he died there long ago, but the 'he' of this sentence is the actual A. R. Sands. The demigod of that name, like the imams of certain Islamic sects or like a prophet of the Old Testament whose name I've forgotten, has gone into occultation and will one day come again to lead his followers in the ways of righteousness.

7. Miss Valora and Pat Tully

IN 1958 AND 1959, I gave more of my time to racing than I had given before or have been able to give since. Those were the two years when I was aged nineteen and twenty and a student at a primary teachers' college. They were also the last years when I lived with my parents and the last years before I began to drink alcohol. I had ample free time. My training course demanded little of me, and I had no girlfriend or social life. My parents didn't even have a television set. I spent most evenings in my room reading. Occasionally, I tried to write poetry. Early in the week, I read what might be called, for convenience, literature. On Thursday and Friday evenings, after the fields for the Saturday races had been published, I read form guides. On Saturday evenings, after the races had been run, I brooded over the results, trying to learn from my successes and failures.

The years mentioned were the only years when I tried to pick winners after having taken into account every available bit of information about every horse. In another section of this book, I explain my lifelong interest in so-called systems or betting methods. One of the attractions of that way of betting is that it demands little time, and for most of my life I've struggled for the time that I would have liked to devote to racing. On those long evenings in 1958 and 1959, however, in my room in Legon Road, South Oakleigh, I treated every race as a unique event and believed I could predict its outcome if only I weighed up every contributing factor or, at least, every factor that I was aware of.

During the years mentioned, I was also something of a conspiracy theorist, perhaps too much influenced as a boy by my father's reports of the doings of the smart men of his acquaintance. I believed in what I later took to calling the paranoid theory of racing. According to this theory, every favoured horse that fails to win has been deliberately prevented from doing so and every outsider that wins, far from surprising its connections, has brought to fruition a detailed plan devised months earlier. As a believer in this theory, I was more likely to select and to back longer-priced horses than favourites. I was also obliged, while watching races, to look out for horses being ridden coldly, as my father would have put it. If, towards the end of a race, my own fancy was on the way to winning, or, more likely, if I could see that my horse had no chance of winning, I would look at the bunch behind the placegetters, hoping to see a horse that was just having a run, which was another euphemism of my father's.

I was looking thus behind the leading horses in the last race at

Caulfield on a cold afternoon in either late August or early September 1958 when I saw Miss Valora (Red, white quarters and sleeves). My vantage point at Caulfield in those days was the unroofed top deck of the huge red-brick grandstand in the Guineas enclosure. (Both the grandstand and the enclosure have been long since done away with.) From where I stood, I looked down on the horses as they passed the furlong marker, about two hundred metres from the winning post. The rider of Miss Valora, the capable but unfashionable Ian Saunders, had moved the mare to the outside of the field in order to give her a clear run at the leaders, or so it might have appeared to a watcher in the main grandstand near the winning post. Looking downwards, and having a rear view of the horses as they approached the post, I saw that Ian Saunders was making only a token effort to urge his mount forward. He flapped his elbows and bobbed his head, but his legs were motionless and he made no use of his whip. If the stewards had questioned him afterwards, Ian Saunders might have said that his mount was tiring, but even I could see that she was going at least as strongly as those around her. If Miss Valora had been ridden hard, she would have gone close to winning but she finished mid-field, and I had no doubt that this was where she had been intended to finish.

The odds bet against Miss Valora on that day at Caulfield were about fifteen-to-one. If her connections backed the mare at her next start, which I supposed was the plan, they might get twice those odds, though this, of course, did not improve her chance of winning. I had previously followed horses with form like Miss Valora's but not always profitably. On the cold afternoon at Caulfield, I merely added the mare to my mental list of horses to be backed at their next start.

During all the years when a public holiday was observed in Melbourne for the Royal Show, a well-attended race meeting was held at Caulfield on that day, which was a Thursday in late September. On the Wednesday before that meeting in 1958, I was approached by a fellow student at the teachers' college, a young man named Lawrie Quinlan. I hardly knew Lawrie, but he was a friendly, outgoing fellow and I could not refuse the favour that he asked of me. Lawrie was going to the races at Caulfield next day. He was taking a young woman student from our college. It would be their first outing together. Her name was Pat Tully.

I took out just now from one of my archives the college magazines from each of the two years that I spent at the teachers' college. I found Pat Tully in two class photos: a tiny black-and-white figure among fifty others. Neither image gave rise to any recollection of any dealings that I ever had with Pat. And yet, I recall that her hair was flame red: the same striking colour as the hair of another student that I had no dealings with. This was a young woman that I would meet again five years later and would take to the Caulfield races and would later be married to for forty-three years.

Lawrie Quinlan told me that he and Pat Tully knew hardly anything about racing. He asked me to write for him a list of horses to back at Caulfield the next day. I took out the racing page of the newspaper for that day and obliged him. I explained that I would not be making *my* final selections until the following morning but that the horses I named for him were among those I ranked most highly.

I marked Miss Valora in the last race but made no special mention of her. I intended to back her but my confidence was lessened by her odds. Bookmakers were preparing to offer twenty-five-to-one against her.

I spent the afternoon of the race meeting in the cheap Guineas enclosure. Lawrie had told me he was lashing out and taking Pat into the costly Grandstand enclosure. For most of the day I hoped Lawrie had not backed my horses; none of them won, although two were placed as less than lucrative odds. In the last race, I had on Miss Valora my standard bet of those days: ten shillings each way. Her odds were thirty-three-to-one; she was a neglected outsider. I risked a pound in order to win about twenty if she won and about five if she ran second or third. She was ridden not by the journeyman-jockey Saunders but by Reg Heather. My father learned later from his acquaintances in the know that Heather actually owned Miss Valora. This would have been against the rules of racing but was quite likely. Owner or not, Reg Heather put much more vigour into his riding than had Ian Saunders on the previous occasion. The mare finished full of running down the outside and won easily.

Lawrie was effusive with his thanks the next day at college. He told me he had bet a pound win-only on each of my selections and had therefore lost seven pounds before Miss Valora's race was run. He had backed her at thirty-three-to-one and had finished the day with a profit of twenty-six pounds: about thirteen hundred dollars in today's currency. He had celebrated by taking Pat Tully to a city hotel for dinner. (The younger reader may not credit it, but Melbourne had hardly any restaurants in the 1950s—cafés, yes, and a few expensive and cliquish old places run by Italian families in upper Bourke or Collins streets, but few of the sorts of restaurants or bistros that abound today.)

Lawrie's successful day had a downside for me (that expression was something else that hadn't come into existence in 1958). Lawrie had decided that I was a master tipster, and every Friday for weeks afterwards I had to give him my selections for the Melbourne meeting on the following day. This was three years before the opening of the first TAB agencies, and so Lawrie probably didn't back my selections but merely checked them against the results in the Saturday evening *Sporting Globe*. He would have lost money if he *had* backed them. Selecting horses for someone else to back is an uncomfortable and thankless task. A Miss Valora comes along only once or twice each year.

If I met up with Lawrie Quinlan during the fifty years following 1958, I have no recollection of it. I certainly met up with him in 2009 and learned from him the detail that completes this section of this book. Certain diligent persons had arranged a reunion, fifty years onwards, for the students who graduated from Toorak Teachers' College in 1959. I had never previously been to any sort of reunion. I suspected that those who attended such functions wanted to boast of their wealth or their achievements. I'm not sorry that I attended the reunion of my old teachers' college, although I had to shut my ears to a certain amount of boasting. No one had achieved great wealth as a result of his or her lifelong career in the Ministry of Education, but those who had stuck it out to the end enjoyed lucrative pensions from their old-fashioned defined-benefits superannuation schemes. What they most often boasted of was their travelling—they seemed to travel every year to some or another far part of the globe. (No one asked me, but if they had I would cheerfully have admitted that I had never been in an aeroplane or on an ocean-going vessel and that I had cashed in my superannuation contributions in 1974 when I resigned from the Education Department, as it was then called, and had used the money as my betting bank during my brief attempt to live as a professional punter.)

Another thing that I noticed about my old fellow students was their abstemiousness. Some drank only water; most drank one or two glasses of wine. The management of the hotel—heaven knows why—had employed three young persons to man the bar in the private-functions area where the reunion took place, and the three stood mostly idle all afternoon. Only Lawrie Quinlan, two other men and I went regularly to the bar for pots of beer. We four supposed that the many hearty beer drinkers we had known at teachers' college had failed to attend because they had drunk themselves into either penury or early graves.

Of course, Lawrie and I recalled Miss Valora's win on Show Day in 1958, and of course I asked if anything had come of his interest in Pat Tully. He told me that they had gone out together only once or twice after their day at Caulfield and that he had not seen her again after they had left teachers' college. He told me, though, that he had heard long ago that Pat had left teaching after a few years and had joined a strict order of nuns.

At the time when Pat Tully had gone off to be a nun, a person entering a convent or a monastery or a seminary was said to have a vocation. Such a person would sometimes admit to having made all at once and unexpectedly the momentous discovery that he or she was called by God to turn aside from worldly concerns and to follow Him. In the days after the reunion, I put together, with hardly any facts to build on, an imaginary account of Pat Tully's discovering her vocation. I was aware of all the social changes that had taken place in the previous fifty years. I was aware that Pat Tully might have long since left her convent, might have been twice married and divorced, and might then have moved to an ashram in India. I understood this, but I choose nowadays, whenever I think of Lawrie Quinlan and Pat Tully, to think of the flame-haired young woman as having turned away forever from worldly concerns after her experience as a racegoer at Caulfield on Show Day in 1958.

Sometimes I suppose that Pat Tully looked around her after the running of the last race of the day and had an insight into the pettiness of what she might have called the material world. She saw the discarded betting tickets littering the ground around her and the dejection on the faces of most of the home-going punters. Even when her escort for the day counted out in front of her the thirty-four pounds he had just then collected from a bookmaker, she felt a sort of pity for the well-meaning young man who could find such satisfaction in a matter so little connected with the salvation of his immortal soul.

Sometimes, however, I imagine that Pat Tully never afterwards forgot the ecstatic moment when the young man who had spent so much effort and so much money in order to have her entertained for the day and who felt, perhaps, a romantic attraction to her— the ecstatic moment when the young man beside her gripped her hand and pointed her fingers towards one of a dozen and more satin-jacketed horsemen bearing down on her from the far distance, and when the increasing prominence of a red-and-white quartered jacket told her that Miss Valora was about to reach the lead; that her lightly made prayer of a few minutes before was about to be answered emphatically; that it was indeed possible for the agencies of the invisible world to intervene in the workings of the visible.

8. *The Two Maikais*

I NEVER MET anyone whose interest in racing matched my own. Both on and off the course, so to speak, I've enjoyed the company of many a racing acquaintance. I've read books, or parts of books, by persons who might have come close to being true racing friends of mine if ever we had met. For most of my long life, however, my enjoyment of racing has been a solitary thing: something I could never wholly explain to anyone else. I've met a few persons with an interest in racing no less intense than mine, but the key word in my opening sentence above is *matched*. Racing has many sides to it, some of them of great interest to me and others of less interest. I have little interest in breeding or pedigrees, for example, but I take a great interest in racing colours and in the naming of horses. In later sections of this book, I'll look further into my lifelong obsession with racing. Here,

I'll simply say that I've never met, in person or through reading, anyone who responds to racing in quite the way that I respond.

My first racing acquaintance was Dennis Hanrahan, who sat in the same classroom with me for three years in the early 1950s. In 1957, soon after we had both left school, Dennis and I began going to every Saturday meeting in Melbourne. For several years, we could afford to go only into the cheaper enclosures. We watched every race together from our agreed vantage points on the Hill at Flemington, on the South Hill at Moonee Valley, and in the Guineas at Caulfield. In fact, we graduated to the Guineas at Caulfield after about a year. Before that, we went to the even cheaper Flat, where the patrons were mostly pensioners or persons of modest means or minors such as ourselves. Dennis and I each had a pair of binoculars bought from the first shipment of Japanese optical instruments to reach Australia after the Second World War. We were almost the only persons in the cheap enclosures to have binoculars and to be able to follow each race in detail. We knew the colours carried by every horse at every meeting and we each murmured a rudimentary call as we watched each race. In those days, when the crowd at a Saturday meeting numbered never less than twenty thousand, the roar from the grandstands often drowned out the words of the course broadcaster, and Dennis and I, in the hubbub after a field had passed the winning post, were often asked by those around us to announce the placegetters to them, which we were always able to do—sometimes before the official numbers were raised above the judge's box. Years later, Dennis became the judge for the Victoria Amateur Turf Club (VATC), which conducted meetings at Caulfield and Sandown.

Mention of race calling prompts me to digress. I believe most callers waste far too many words in an effort to describe details better left to the imagination of the listener. This is especially so with course broadcasters, whose audience can usually make out with their own eyes the string of distant horse shapes and need only to be told such facts as that the leader is so-and-so, while the horse going forward on the outside is so-and-so...Even callers addressing radio audiences try needlessly for descriptive language when simpler terms would do. For example, the word *tiring* alone conveys enough to me, and yet callers describe horses as *stopping to a walk* or *falling in a hole* or *feeling the pinch*...The American term *closing* alone would supply me with an image of a horse likely soon to reach the lead. I don't need to be told that a certain runner is *coming with a well-timed run* or *emerging from the pack*, not to mention *finishing like a shot out of a gun* or *coming from the clouds*...

By far the best race caller I ever heard was Geoff Mahoney, who called the Sydney races for the ABC for thirty years, from the late 1950s until the late 1980s. In his *History of Australian Thoroughbred Racing*, Andrew Lemon quotes a description of Mahoney as having 'superb control, impeccable diction and a style as smooth as velvet'. When reporting a close finish, most race callers raise their voices or shout. Mahoney used not volume but tone and pitch whenever a blanket finish threatened—even in a Doncaster Handicap or a Golden Slipper. I never heard Mahoney stumble over a horse's name or offer a gratuitous comment on anything he observed. He avoided even the use of first names for trainers or jockeys. Most callers seem to use these to suggest that they, the callers, are matey with the big names of racing. Mahoney was the only caller who never referred to the famous Sydney trainer as *Tommy Smith*. To Geoff Mahoney, the man was always *T. J. Smith*.

By far the worst caller I ever heard was Bert Bryant, who has often been named by persons who should know better as having been one of the best. Bryant began calling in his teens in the district around Dubbo, New South Wales, and became assistant caller at 3UZ in Melbourne in 1948, when he was in his early twenties. I would never deny that Bryant was a most capable caller in his first years at 3UZ but he soon afterwards began to turn into a self-opinionated loudmouth, and by the end of his career he was an incompetent buffoon and I could hardly bear to listen to him.

For many years, I owned a long-playing recording of Bert Bryant's calls of the Melbourne Cup from about 1950 until 1960. Even during those ten years, his calls of the Cup gave evidence of his decline. In his early years, he was fluent and impersonal. In later years, it was easy to tell which horse he himself had backed, and not just because it was favourite but because of the inordinate trouble he took to report on its prospects during the running. Not only that, but he tried more and more to put into his calls what his admirers praised as colourful description but I considered time-wasting and foolish. Often, he would report that a horse running wide was hanging out or sticking out like granny's tooth or that a horse showing unexpected stamina was staying on like a mother-in-law.

Most callers in their later years deliver too many of their own opinions and prejudices but Bryant was unrelenting. One day in the 1960s, a horse named Nyngan (some or other combination of black, gold, and pale blue) seemed likely to win a staying race at Moonee Valley. Now, the same horse had disappointed his followers on several recent occasions, starting favourite and finishing no better than third or fourth. No doubt, Bryant had been one of those followers but had not backed the horse on the day that I'm writing about. When Nyngan reached the lead in the straight, Bryant came out with, 'Don't tell me the dog's going to win a race at last! Yes, Nyngan wins it! The dog wins it!' I was told later that the owners of Nyngan demanded and received an apology from Bryant for his remarks, and rightly so.

Bert Bryant was a profoundly ignorant man who took no interest in the meanings of obscure names or the approximate pronunciation of foreign names. One day he wondered aloud about the meaning of the name Guid Gillie. An obliging listener phoned the studio at 3UZ to say that the name meant 'good gamekeeper'. Bryant seemed not only to have no acquaintance with Scots dialect words but also not to know what a gamekeeper might be. He interpreted the phrase as *good, game keeper*, and then resorted to his excruciating brand of lame humour. '*Good, game keeper*,' he mused aloud. 'Why, that must mean *husband*!'

Bryant was at his absolute worst one day at Warrnambool in May 1974, when he was calling not only for listeners on the radio but for the big crowd on course as well. Rain was falling, the track was heavy, and jockeys' colours were spattered with mud as the field in the first race came up the straight. Yes, conditions were difficult, but celebrity race callers such as Bryant are paid generous salaries in return for their coping with such things. A hundred metres short of the post, about six horses were vying for the lead—another difficulty, but surely not insurmountable for a man of Bryant's reputation. As the expression goes, Bryant lost it. He spluttered and blurted out not so much racehorse names as cries of 'I don't know where to look!' or 'There's half the field spread across the track!' It was the worst call of a finish that I had ever heard, and if a young caller-on-probation had been responsible for it he would surely have lost his job.

Worse was to come. Bryant had obviously no idea of the identity of the winner and, after he had filled in with fatuous chat, the numbers appeared outside the judge's box. Bryant announced the winner's name, which I've long since forgotten. Then came a pause. Now, the rider of the winner appeared in the race book as *S. Buhagiar*. Sam Buhagiar had ridden for years in the south-west of Victoria and the south-east of South Australia, with much success. He had ridden occasionally in Melbourne, where Bryant would have been calling. Perhaps Bert was still discomposed by his failure to call the recent finish. Perhaps he was still hung over from his drinking into the early hours of that morning. (The three-day May Carnival at Warrnambool was renowned for the drinking that went on in every hotel between Camperdown and Port Fairy. My mother spent the last forty years of her life in Warrnambool, and she and her cronies provided me several times with anecdotal evidence— gossip, if you prefer—about the drinking feats of Bert Bryant and his offsider, John Russell.) I mentioned a pause back there. After the pause, Bert Bryant blurted out that the rider of the winner was *S. Boomerang*! Someone in his vicinity must have rebuked him at once, or perhaps even Bryant himself began to understand what a fool he was making of himself. He came out with the absurd explanation: 'I don't know the lad.' Only four years later, Bryant announced his early retirement from race calling. His stated reason was ill health. He should have been induced to retire many years earlier on the grounds of his gross incompetence. The digression has now ended.

I have a lasting memory of Dennis Hanrahan from a day at Flemington in the early 1960s. He and I were on the old Hill, watching the finish of a weight-for-age race. Three outstanding horses were fighting out the finish. Dennis would have backed one or another of the three; he could never watch a race without having a small bet on it, although he had to give up betting when he was appointed assistant judge for the VATC. But betting was always for Dennis and me only a small part of the marvellous pageant of racing. When the leaders were about fifty metres from the finish and the result was still impossible to predict, I heard Dennis say—not to me but to himself, and in the same tone that he and I as Catholic schoolboys had formerly used for our prayers in classroom and chapel—'Racing at its best!'

David Walton is my oldest friend. We met up in the school ground at De La Salle College, Malvern, in February 1952, when we were both in short trousers. David's father was a bookmaker, but David seemed uninterested in racing during our schooldays. He and his wife, Yvonne, spent more than twenty years in the Middle East and, after their return to Australia in the early 1990s, they and my wife, Catherine, and I sat together in the members' stands of all four Melbourne racecourses on almost every Saturday until my wife was no longer able to go to the races. What most unites David and me as racegoers is our interest in the *people* at the races. I have seen David sometimes turn away for a moment from watching a field of horses in the straight in order to watch a nearby person or a group of persons that he knows to be among the owners of one of the horses. Likewise, when most spectators are watching the winning horse and rider returning across the mounting yard, David will have his binoculars trained on the stalls at the edge of the yard where the owners and trainers of the placegetters, each in his or her unique way, register elation or ruefulness or downright disappointment. In the language of pop psychology, David is trying to relate to the people around the stalls or to empathise with them. In the language of his and my childhood, the language that I call backstreet Australian, he is stickybeaking. It's a harmless but salutary exercise, and I join him in it often, even if our other racing interests don't always coincide.

Timothy Doyle and I went to the races together every Saturday during the late 1980s, and we still meet occasionally at Caulfield. Timothy appreciates most of the pleasures of racing but nothing as much as backing a winner at long odds. If it were permitted to write doctoral theses on topics related to racing, Tim would have written long ago, and would have been awarded first-class honours for, a thesis with the title *Form Reversals: The tendency among favourites that have run unplaced subsequently to return to winning form at longer odds, and the degree of predictability of this phenomenon of the turf.* Tim is ever alert to the humour of racing, but he and I did not meet until I was well past forty, and I find it hard to share with him many of my formative experiences from my early years as a racegoer.

Because my surname is Irish, some people have foolishly described me as an Irish-Australian, whatever that might be. Of my eight great-grandparents, the only Irish person was the man whose surname I've inherited. The other seven were all English—and Protestant, if they were anything. I was much more influenced as a boy by my father's relatives than by my mother's, but the Murnane men were far from resembling the square-jawed cartoon Irishmen who brawl and booze and burst often into sentimental song. My father and his brothers were teetotallers who neither smoked nor swore nor told off-colour jokes. If not for their interest in racing, they could have been called Catholic wowsers. Even their talkativeness and their wittiness came more, I suspect, from their mother, a Mansbridge with a Sussex father, than from dour Thomas Murnane, their father, who was, in any case, only half-Irish himself.

My favourite among my father's brothers was the youngest, Louis. I probably confided more to my uncle Louis than to my own father. I certainly talked much more about racing with Louis than with my father, who became more and more distracted in his later years by his mounting debts and his efforts to recoup them by betting. I grew apart from Louis in his later years and was estranged from him after he took offence at the two books of mine that were published during his lifetime, although we shook hands on his deathbed. Fictional versions of my favourite uncle are in several of my books. Even thirty years after his death, when I was writing *Barley Patch*, I was driven yet again to fictionalise him.

Louis and I were great racing friends, but there were definite limits to what we could share. At one time in the late 1950s or the early 1960s, a young apprentice rider named Ricky Chrisp was listed in form guides. I doubt whether he rode more than a few winners and, like most apprentice jockeys, he was driven out of racing by increasing weight or decreasing opportunities. One morning, while I was poring over the results of the previous day's races at Woodend or Pakenham, I was amused to see Ricky's surname printed as *Christ*. I saw Louis only a few times yearly, but I knew that he, like myself, read the racing results carefully every day. When I next visited Louis in Warrnambool, I reminded him of the misprinted version of the apprentice's name. He gave a nervous smile, and I should have left the matter there. Instead I went well beyond the unspoken bounds of our racing friendship, and I still cringe when I recall the discomfort I caused him. I said something to the effect that I had always been prepared for the Second Coming of our Saviour but that I was most surprised at His returning not in glory but as an untalented apprentice jockey.

My wife, Catherine, rode ponies as a girl, although she had no contact with horses in later years. We were not able to go regularly together to the races until after our three sons had reached their teens and Catherine had taken early retirement. We made up for her lost racing opportunities by going together to most Melbourne meetings during the last fifteen years before her health failed in 2006. Catherine loved to immerse herself in the details of the form guide. She would devote twenty minutes at least to selecting the horse that would carry her ten-dollar bet in each forthcoming race and when, as sometimes happened, her selection won at good odds, she would suppose she had discovered at last her own selection method. What I never understood about Catherine was her utter lack of interest in racing when she was not at her table in the members' lounge of a Saturday afternoon, studying her form guide, or in the grandstand watching race after race. I never saw her look at the racing pages of a newspaper in our house. She never asked to accompany me on my many trips to our local TAB agency. She enjoyed being a racegoer, but for six days of the week she spared no thought for racing, whereas I walked often in a fog of racing memories and racing possibilities.

I tried once or twice to acquire a new racing friend; to convert to my way of life someone who seemed peculiarly in sympathy with me in fields other than racing. When *Tamarisk Row* was published in 1974, a man I had never heard of wrote in a newspaper review that the book was the best he had read for many years. I later met up with him, and we became good friends. His name was John Tittensor. He was perhaps my closest friend for ten years, until he left Australia after the death of his two children in a house fire. One day, encouraged by the close affinity that we seemed to share, I told John the story of the two Maikais.

In the Great Age of Racing, betting on horses was almost the only legal form of gambling in Victoria. In those years, the nearest equivalent to the lotto draws of today was doubles betting on the Caulfield and Melbourne cups or the Doncaster Handicap and the Sydney Cup or a few other pairs of notable races. Specially licensed doubles bookmakers posted every few weeks to their clients detailed charts showing the odds against many thousands of combinations of horses in the two designated races. Even the combination of the favourite in each race might be quoted at a hundred-to-one, while a pair of outsiders could be backed at odds of ten thousand-to-one or even more. Bookmakers were able to offer these seemingly generous odds because no refunds were made for scratchings. In July, when the first charts were issued for the Caulfield and Melbourne cups, the entrants for each race numbered several hundreds. Hardly more than twenty started in each race. All the money wagered on the hundreds of scratched horses stayed in the bookmakers' pools.

In the winter of 1939, when I was a babe-in-arms, my father's smart racing mates were informed by others of their kind in Western

Australia that a horse named Maikai (colours unknown), which was little known even in its home state, was being prepared to win both the Caulfield Cup and the Melbourne Cup. My father at the time was a warder at Pentridge Prison, with a weekly wage of perhaps five pounds. He trusted the smart men in the west enough, or he was foolhardy enough, to bet two pounds on the two Maikais, which was the expression used for the combination of the same horse in each of two feature races. Maikai was a rank outsider in each race, and my father stood to win forty thousand pounds.

In the following months, Maikai performed just as his stable had expected. He won several major handicaps in Western Australia and was one of the better-fancied runners in the Caulfield Cup. The pain suffered by the followers of Maikai on Caulfield Cup Day would have been severe indeed, but worse was to come. Maikai ran second in the Caulfield Cup to the mare Rivette (Black, rose diamonds and cap). All bets were, of course, lost, but what would the Maikai camp have felt on Melbourne Cup Day when their horse again finished a close second to Rivette? Just the one rival had thwarted a once-in-a-lifetime coup. Had Rivette not started in the cups, my father might have lived afterwards from the rents of a street of terrace houses rather than a prison warder's wages.

I told this story once to John Tittensor. I'm sure I mentioned enough background details for him to grasp the full import. To judge from his comment afterwards, he had got my general drift, as they say, but I learned from that same comment that John was one more of the many intelligent, imaginative persons I've known for whom racing is a closed book.

Said John: 'If only your poor father had backed it each way!'

9. *Illoura and Miss Lawler*

DURING THE SEVEN years between my leaving school and my meeting up with the young woman who was later my wife for forty-three years, I had only three girlfriends, and the total length of time during which I was thus provided was about six months. During the other six and a half years, I was a solitary. In my solitary periods, I went out once or, at most, twice with each of five young women. During the same periods, I invited each of three other young women to go out with me but was turned down. All this seemed rather dispiriting at the time, and yet I was aware even then of a sort of paradox in my romantic life, if it deserves to have been so called.

During the long periods when I was solitary and without a girlfriend, I considered myself deprived, and my prevailing mood was a sort of low-grade misery. And yet, my state of mind whenever

I *had* a girlfriend, or while I was trying to acquire one, was no sort of improvement on the earlier state of mind and not at all what I had hoped for. The advantage of my being solitary was that things were settled and predictable. I read more and wrote more as a solitary and was able to become accustomed to my gloomy moods. Whenever I had a girlfriend, I lived in a permanent state of uncertainty. Even my free time was mostly given to wondering and speculating: what were her true feelings towards me? how long would it be before we fell out? But the worst hardship that my three short-term girlfriends caused was my enforced absence from the races during our time together. I felt obliged to go out with each girlfriend every Saturday night. This in itself was a strain: I could seldom think of anything better than to go with her to some or another tedious film and to drink an over-priced cup of coffee with her afterwards in some pretentious so-called coffee lounge. I needed to conserve my nervous energy of a Saturday afternoon and, sometimes, to be ready early in the evening if we were to have a meal together before our outing. I was obliged to stay at home every Saturday afternoon and to listen to radio broadcasts of the Melbourne races, often without being able to have a bet.

I can distinctly recall each of the three occasions when I went to the races for the first time after an enforced absence caused by my involvement with a girlfriend. My two or three racing acquaintances made no fuss over me, but I felt as though each detail of my surroundings had acquired an aura or radiance as though to remind me that racing had remained true to me, even though I had thought to desert it for the sake of some foolish illusion.

The first of my three returns to racing took place in September

1957, the second in March 1960, and the third in February 1964. This section of this book is concerned with the second of the three. I lost the first and the third of my girlfriends as a result of *their* deciding to end our association. My parting from the second of the three could be described as having been by mutual consent. My first day back at the races was the Australian Cup meeting at Flemington on Monday, 7 March, which was a public holiday. In Melbourne during March, the sunlight has a quality that has always affected me strangely. The harshness of the summer light has been somehow altered. Distant scenery appears as though under glass. Something in the air promises me answers to questions that have for long teased me. (I wonder whether my becoming unsettled by the sunlight in March is connected with my first exposure to sun and sky. I was born in late February. In the earliest photograph of me, I lie in a cane bassinet under a gauzy cloth on a patch of lawn behind the boarding house in Breese Street, Brunswick, that was my parents' home at the time. The month would have been March or April.) Even if I had not been still affected by the loss of my second girlfriend, I would have derived a bitter-sweetness from the notable sunlight on Australian Cup Day, 1960.

The Australian Cup was not then what it is nowadays. In 1960, it was still one of the longest feature races in Australia, with a distance of about 3500 metres in today's measurements. The start was at the top of the straight-six course, about three hundred metres behind the Melbourne Cup start. The average field for the Australian Cup included few horses of the sort that contested the Melbourne Cup. Runners in the longer race were moderate stayers and there were even a few hurdlers. My selection in 1960 was a moderate stayer indeed, the gelding Illoura (Black, yellow braces and sleeves).

I had been following the races as best I could during my brief involvement with my second girlfriend. I had marked Illoura as a horse to follow after he had run a disappointing race at Moonee Valley soon after having won convincingly a race for stayers at the same course. I supposed he was being prepared to win again at good odds in a field of average quality, and I was most surprised when I saw his name in the field for the Australian Cup. Bookmakers seemed to share my opinion of his chances; they were offering thirty-three-to-one against him. I was not at all confident but I bet thirty shillings on Illoura at forty-to-one.

I watched the race in exquisite autumn sunshine from high in the old Hill reserve. Illoura was ridden by Frank Treen, who had settled in Melbourne after having been a leading rider in Perth. I respected Treen as a rider but I muttered against him when he took Illoura to the lead early in the race. At the far side of the course, Illoura was ten lengths in front of the nearest horse, and I could not believe he would last the distance. But Frank Treen was a masterly judge of pace. He confused the other riders by varying the speed of his mount, which was what journalists call a plodding stayer. When the field turned for home, Illoura was still ten lengths in front. I waited with dread for the plodder to tire. At the clock tower, Illoura was spent, but when I looked back I saw that the others were no less so. At the winning post, Illoura could hardly lift his legs, but he was still six lengths clear, and the brave plodder had won me the equivalent of four weeks' salary.

I was in my first year as a primary teacher, a temporary assistant at Doveton, a newly built outer suburb of Housing Commission homes on the edge of Dandenong. Conditions at the school were trying for teachers, but the staff were exceptionally friendly and helpful to one another. Few young teachers could afford cars at that time, and the senior male assistant, Leo Dobrigh, saved a young woman and me hours of travel on public transport by picking us up and dropping us off in our respective suburbs, which were on his route. Each Friday afternoon, he parked his late-model Holden outside one of the hotels in the main street in Dandenong. The young woman remained in the back seat, preparing the weekly work program that every primary teacher was compelled to maintain, while Leo and I drank four glasses of beer with Jack McLachlan, the head teacher of Doveton, and Brian Brady, one of the male assistants.

I had grown up knowing nothing of alcohol and had drunk my first glass of beer only a few months before my arrival at Doveton. I was twenty-one, while the youngest of my three colleagues and drinking mates, Brian Brady, would have been at least twice my age. Even four glasses of beer, drunk rapidly on an empty stomach, was enough to make me cheerful and talkative. Not only the beer affected me; by Friday afternoon, I had studied the fields for the Melbourne races on the Saturday and was full of pleasant anticipation. Moreover, Australian Cup Day had been the first of a sequence of winning days. On the third or fourth Friday after Illoura's win, my lack of a girlfriend caused me no feeling of deprivation. Racing and I seemed to have reached an amicable understanding.

On that Friday afternoon, whichever day it was, I must have told my three fellow drinkers that I had no girlfriend. I don't recall having done so, but I recall their discussing with mock-seriousness which of the single women teachers at Doveton would be the most suitable girlfriend for me. They had much fun arguing for and against the suitability of even the middle-aged or the ill-favoured. They settled at last on the young woman who was sitting just then in the rear of Leo Dobrigh's car. Her name was Dorothy Lawler, and she seemed to be about my own age. I had found her pleasant company in the car but had never felt attracted to her or sensed that she found me of interest. The last thing I recall from our time in the bar that afternoon is Leo's suddenly seeming to become serious and his urging me to approach Dorothy, who was, so he assured me, a good-hearted girl who lived with her widowed mother and had no serious boyfriend.

I can give no clear account of what followed, let alone of my reasons for doing as I did. I've drunk a great deal of beer since 1960, with little harm to my health or reputation, but I could wish that I had not said some of the things that I said while drinking or, more precisely, some of the things that I seem to recall having said. I seem to recall from that afternoon while Leo Dobrigh drove Dorothy Lawler and me from Dandenong to Caulfield, where I was dropped off, my being asked how I was going to spend the coming weekend. If I *was* asked this, it must surely have been Leo who asked, his intention being to break down the reserve between Dorothy and myself. If I was *not* asked this, then the four glasses of beer had made me reckless indeed, for I recall my delivering to Leo and Dorothy a short lecture, the title of which might well have been 'Racing as a Complete Way of Life' and the subject matter of which might well have included such assertions as that a young man who devoted himself to racing was content to rest quietly at home of a Saturday evening and that such a young man got from racing at least as much satisfaction and fulfilment as other young men got from going with other young persons to picture theatres or coffee lounges or dances or parties.

If I never afterwards recalled the exact words of my short lecture, still I recalled that I delivered it in a tone of mock-formality and made needless use of long words. I recalled also that I contrived to address Dorothy Lawler at least once during the lecture and not by her first name, as I usually addressed her, but as *Miss Lawler*. This was not quite as inelegant as it might seem nowadays. Dorothy and I were not long out of teachers' college, where lecturers addressed eighteen-years-old students as *Miss This* or *Mister That*. District inspectors used the same form of address when conferring with teachers they had not previously met. And even teachers from the same school addressed each other thus in the hearing of students. But why did I thus address the girl I greeted as *Dorothy* each morning in Leo's car? More to the point, why did I deliver the lecture in the first place?

Perhaps I was trying to rebuke Leo for his clumsy attempt at matchmaking. Perhaps I supposed that Dorothy just may have been interested in me. (I was as inept then as I am still today at interpreting the language and behaviour of others, especially females.) If so, then my lecture would have been meant to explain to her why her interest was not returned. Or, was I secretly appealing to Dorothy? Was I informing her that I was without a girlfriend, just as she, for the time being, was without a boyfriend, and that she had only to tell me in the car that afternoon, or next week in the school corridor, that she had never been to a race meeting and would like to learn how horse racing could have such an attraction for a person such as myself? Nudge, nudge; wink, wink, as they used to say long ago.

Whatever my motives might have been (and I'm hardly better at interpreting my own behaviour than that of others), my lecture achieved nothing, although Leo never afterwards recommended Dorothy to me. I recall that an awkward silence followed the lecture. If I was embarrassed in front of Leo and Dorothy during later days, my embarrassment would have been short-lived. My position at Doveton was only temporary. I was liable to be moved elsewhere at short notice by the clerks in the teachers' branch of the Education Department, and a few weeks after my lecture I was moved far away indeed. Although I remained a teacher for eight more years and after that a publications officer in the Education Department for five years, I never again saw any of my former colleagues from what I think of as the Illoura period of my life.

10. *Form-Plan and Otto Fenichel*

IN THE LONG-AGO 1960s, I knew a man who claimed to have been helped though a troubled period by his faith in psychoanalysis. When I myself was going through such a period, he urged me to read a certain huge book on the subject. I've forgotten the title but I recall the author's name, which was in gilt letters on the dark-green spine: Otto Fenichel. I read several chapters but I recall today only two short passages. One passage described the symptoms of a man with an obsessive-compulsive disorder. He could never walk more than a few paces forward without obeying an urge to look behind him for any beetle that was lying helpless on its back and needing to be set upright. The other passage was the opening sentence of a section on gambling. According to the learned author, the gambler gambles in order to learn whether or not God has forgiven him for his masturbation. This may or may not be so, but it provides me with an excellent opening to a discussion of systematic ways of betting, or systems, as they used to be called for short. If Fenichel or his followers had ever learned how much time and effort I've put into my search for a reliable and profitable betting system, they could only have concluded that I was either the all-time champion Onanist or, at least, the one of all the practitioners of the ancient art who felt the most guilty about it.

I wish I could recall what first led me to investigate betting systems. In my early years as a follower of racing, I tried to pick winners haphazardly, but in 1952, when I was only thirteen, I began recording the recent form of every winner, hoping to discover some recurrent pattern that would help me predict future winners. In all my life, I've never bought a ticket in a lottery or any sort of lotto game with huge prizes. I've always believed the odds to be too much against me. And yet, I still today continue the research that I began as a boy more than sixty years ago; I still spend a few minutes each morning checking the results of the latest betting system that I've devised.

If I were to find my golden goose this year, I would make no effort to profit from it. My wants are simple nowadays, and I live in frugal comfort. If my lifetime of research should be rewarded at last, my only pleasure, apart from my knowledge of God's forgiveness, would come from my leaving the details of my discovery in the folder where I store my Last Will and my instructions for my funeral service. None of my sons shares my obsession with the turf, but all of them would surely be grateful for my leaving them the means for earning a supplementary income.

Even during the few months in late 1958 and early 1959 when I was sure I had found the Holy Grail of punting, I had no plans for conspicuous consumption. I intended to reinvest my winnings until my betting bank was large enough to supply me with a yearly income of two thousand pounds (about one hundred thousand dollars in today's currency). This income would enable me to rent a comfortable flat in Dandenong Road, Armadale; to own a small car; to join a middle-level golf club; and to put together a library of a few hundred volumes of fiction and poetry, along with a select collection of long-playing records. I had been much impressed by a few paragraphs in a feature article in the *Herald* newspaper about the private lives of rails bookmakers. If anyone had discovered the perfect betting system, these men had. So long as they set their books properly and bet equally against all the favoured horses, they could never lose. Those who agreed to be interviewed for the article all chose to remain anonymous and played down the extent of their wealth but freely discussed their interests apart from racing. Many had farms or businesses, yet the man who most impressed me had installed a massive pipe organ in a large, acoustically sound room in his house. He fielded on the rails every Saturday and public holiday but took no other interest in racing. On most weekdays, he spent several hours alone in his chapel-sized room deep among the tree-shaded streets of Toorak, practising his Bach fugues. My way of life would not be quite so austere as that of the bookmaker-organist; I would study each day the newspaper form guides and the results of the previous day's meetings. However, I would attend the races only when I had to back a horse selected by the strict conditions of my lucrative betting method. On other days, if I wasn't on the fairways of Riversdale or Commonwealth, I was in my upstairs study overlooking Dandenong Road, with one of Sibelius's symphonies sounding in the background while I tried to write a poem in the style of Thomas Hardy.

I should explain that my research into betting systems was mostly theoretical. For much of my life I've selected horses according to my own judgement but with a few guiding principles in mind, although nothing resembling the strict rules of the profitable system that I always hoped to find. For example, I bet with moderate success for many years by selecting a horse at single-figure odds to beat the favourite and then backing both that horse and the favourite, so that the favourite would return me my total outlay if it won, while the other horse would show me a profit. My search for the perfect system took place mostly on Sundays or Wednesdays, when I would spread out in front of me the form guide from the previous Saturday together with the results from either the Saturday evening edition or the Wednesday edition of the *Sporting Globe*. These documents gave me what would be called today instant feedback. Did I want to know how I would have fared on the previous Saturday if I had backed only last-start winners quoted at single-figure odds? I had only to list my hypothetical selections and then to learn their fate from the results in the *Globe*. What if I had backed only those horses ridden for the first time by the leading jockey or by one of the three leading jockeys? The results in the *Globe* gave me my answer within minutes. Nor was I so foolish as to suppose that the worth of a betting system or selection method could be assessed from the results at a single race meeting. I kept form guides and *Globes* for months on end. Although I had not then heard the word, I was conducting *longitudinal* studies of each method that I devised.

I seem to recall that the advertising of betting systems was made illegal at some time since the 1960s, which might explain why no such ads appear nowadays, although some tipsters are apparently free to offer their services. In the late 1950s, when I saw the first ads for Form-Plan, not only the *Sporting Globe* but *Turf Monthly* and other racing publications published ads for systems, mostly boasting results that defied belief and always having as a business address a post-office box in a capital city. I can recall only one system that was advertised continually for year after year; the others disappeared, so to speak, after six months or a year, presumably when disgruntled purchasers had spread the word that their own results failed to match those claimed for past years. Failures of this kind need not prove that the marketer of the system has been downright dishonest. Several times, when looking through past records to check the worth of one of my own systems, I've decided to vary one or another rule so that the system would have selected a certain winner at long odds. I might even have done this more than once, only to learn later that the new rules obliged me to include so many losing selections that the profits from the long-priced horse were wiped out. As financial advisers remind us nowadays, past results may not necessarily be repeated in the future.

I do recall one instance, however, of deliberate deception. The promoter of the system, so I was told, provided purchasers with a plan for backing one or another of the three horses uppermost in the so-called newspaper poll. In those days, several newspapers in both Sydney and Melbourne provided detailed coverage of racing.

This included selections from up to ten tipsters and a poll ranking horses according to their popularity with the tipsters. If the deviser of the system had told purchasers which of the various polls he had used to obtain his lucrative past results, then the results could easily have been checked from old newspapers. But the deviser of the system claimed that each user should make up his or her own poll, using the selections of six or seven so-called leading tipsters. This, he assured his hopeful clients, was what *he* had done in the past. In other words, no one testing the system could claim that certain winners supposedly backed in the past had not been among the top three in any popularity poll; the deviser of the system could simply claim that his own privately assembled poll had most certainly included the said horses. Likewise, if the poor purchaser failed to show a profit from the first few months of betting, he might be told, or he might himself believe, that his choice of tipsters was at fault.

I had been following the races for nearly ten years when Form-Plan was first promoted. As nearly as I can recall, this took place in early 1957. I had seen nothing like it before: a whole page of the Wednesday *Sporting Globe* was given over to advertising a betting method alleged to select about fifty per cent winners and seventy-five per cent placings, and to have turned a modest starting bank into a small fortune during the past five years. Apart from the lavish advertising, what distinguished Form-Plan from all other systems that I had read about was that the man selling Form-Plan was doing so under his own name and from his home address. Well, being somewhat older and wiser now than in 1957, I suppose I should write that the promoter of Form-Plan claimed to be named A. T. Maclean and to live at a stated address in Batman Street, West

Melbourne. As further evidence of his trustworthiness, he provided a likeness of himself—or certainly of a nondescript man looking studiously through horn-rimmed spectacles.

I may be writing ironically now, but all this caused something of a stir among my racing acquaintances, who were used to reading about systems peddled from Sydney post-office boxes. I tried to keep an open mind. I would have liked to believe that someone had at last discovered what I had searched for in vain for nearly ten years. My chief query arose from my frequent daydream of what *I* would do after I had discovered my own equivalent of Form-Plan. The very *last* thing I would do would be to advertise my discovery to the racing public of Victoria and to provide them with a likeness of myself, with or without horn-rimmed glasses.

Connected with this was my fear of what might happen if punters in their hundreds or their thousands bought Mr Maclean's foolproof system and set about using it every Saturday. In fact, part of my concern was that the system could *not* be used every Saturday. It was clear from the summary of results in the advertisement that Form-Plan selected hardly more than twenty horses each year. If someone following the system were to make more than pocket money from it, he or she would have to bet very large sums indeed on each of the small number of selections. The economics of the system, and even of racing in general, might be altered if hundreds, or even thousands, of Form-Plan followers rushed at the book-makers whenever a selection was about to race.

Yes, I had my doubts, and yet a time came when I could hold out no longer. The ads had been appearing in the *Sporting Globe* every week for much more than a year and yet the economics of racing had seemed unchanged. Mr Maclean would have had to sell thousands of copies of his system to pay for his ads and to make a profit. I could only assume that his clients were satisfied with what they had been sold. The horn-rimmed visage still appeared week after week, and I had read no newspaper account of bricks having been thrown through windows in Batman Street, West Melbourne. Perhaps the followers of Form-Plan were content with modest profits and not yet eager to give up their day jobs, as we say nowadays.

Form-Plan cost ten pounds. About a year after I had bought my copy, I began work as a primary teacher near the bottom of the salary scale. My first fortnightly pay cheque amounted to thirty-four pounds. A better comparison might be the cost of a good-quality hardcover book at that time: about one and a half pounds. Mr Maclean's product was at the top end of the market, to use another present-day expression.

I didn't actually pay the full price for Form-Plan. In September 1958, I went halves with a fellow student teacher named Graham Nash, whom I haven't seen or heard of for nearly fifty-five years. Without knowing it, we had bought Form-Plan at the right time. The system selected only two-years-old horses. Races for two-years-old in Melbourne and interstate begin in late September or early October and end in late July. That was our first surprise. From early August we would have nothing to bet on for nearly two months. Nor would our betting be frantic in other months. As the advertised summaries of results had suggested, Form-Plan selected only about twenty horses each year in Melbourne and Sydney combined. This was about one bet each fortnight. I could not easily foresee myself going for two weeks at a time without betting. But I rather admired the selection method itself. Like many other observant punters, I had noticed that races for two-years-old seemed more often won by the favourite or the best-performed horse. I had sometimes skulked around bookmakers' stands when the clerk was working out the final result for a race, and I had learned sometimes from a betting sheet that a race for two-years-old had resulted in a loss for the bookmaker because punters had wanted to back only the favourite or the second-favourite. Form-Plan selected only top weights in two-years-old races, whether or not they were favourites. A selection had to have won or been placed recently. I forget the other few rules, except that selections had to be backed each way, that is, for both a win and a place. I found this puzzling at the time, and I wonder now whether it was a result of the sort of tinkering that I had mentioned earlier: whether Mr Maclean had decided to recommend each-way betting after having noticed at some point in his past results a frustrating sequence of second and third placings.

Graham Nash and I had shared the cost of Form-Plan, but we kept our betting separate. I had decided to bet five pounds each way on each selection, which was several times more than the largest bet I had previously had. On the other hand, I intended to bet only on Form-Plan horses, saving my money for a few decisive bets. The first of them was on a filly named Snowflower (Pale blue, tartan sash) at Caulfield on the Wednesday before the Caulfield Cup. Snowflower was narrowly beaten but that was all right for a start, we thought. We had lost only a quarter of our outlay after collecting on our place bets. Our second bet was ten days later, on Moonee Valley Cup Day, as we used to call the day that is now known as Cox Plate Day. Our selection was the filly that had beaten Snowflower at

Caulfield: Faithful City (Green, gold Maltese cross, striped sleeves and cap). Faithful City was at the generous odds of four-to-one. The favourite was Ritmar (White, purple stripes), a filly from Sydney ridden by Neville Sellwood. I wish I could remember who rode Faithful City. Ritmar could gallop only at top speed, and the rider of Faithful City, having seen this, held his mount together for a last run at the favourite. Ritmar led by two lengths around the turn. The straight at Moonee Valley is short but uphill. Ritmar began to tire and Faithful City to gain ground. Graham and I were in the old South Hill reserve, almost head-on to the finish. We had no idea which filly had won. The judge studied the print of the photo finish for three or four minutes and then declared Faithful City the winner.

I have always maintained that a writer achieves nothing by trying to describe feelings; that feelings can only be suggested. I will therefore report only that my feelings, after Faithful City's narrow win, were mixed. I had in my possession the key to lifelong wealth, but so too had all those numerous unknown buyers of Mr Maclean's method. How long would it be before half the population of Melbourne heard about Form-Plan and flocked to the races to get their share of the easy money?

Our next bet was on Faithful City again, in a race for two-years-old fillies on Melbourne Cup Day. I have no recollection of the Cup, which was won by Baystone (Dark-blue-and-lilac stripes, red cap), but I recall Faithful City leading all the way in the fillies' race. Her odds were short: a bit less than two-to-one, but I had increased my bet to eight pounds each way and had won the equivalent of four times my weekly allowance as a student teacher. I was even more anxious by now when I thought of all the other punters who were winning as I was. How could we all keep winning for month after month and year after year? And yet, I had not overheard at any race meeting a single conversation about Form-Plan. When I had stood in the queues to collect my winnings, no one around me had uttered thanks to Mr Maclean. Perhaps there *were* Form-Plan followers around me waiting to collect, except that they were desperate, as I was, to stop the word from spreading.

Nowadays, I speculate that most of the buyers of Form-Plan were persons such as I was in those days: workers and lowly public servants and small-time punters, all dreaming of their own versions of my leisurely life in Dandenong Road, Armadale. I speculate further that even Form-Plan, successful though it seemed for a time, was not what they had hoped for when they sent off their ten pounds to Mr Maclean. They had wanted lively betting, action, bets in every race, frequent winners at long odds. They could not foresee themselves retiring early as a result of backing twenty two-years-old horses each year at short odds. As for the real punters—the stable commissioners, the likes of Teddy Ettershank, and the bookmakers especially—if they even read the *Sporting Globe*, they would have barely glanced at Mr Maclean's full-page ads. They, the real punters, had seen systems come and go. As a leading bookmaker said to me many years later, 'I like all punters, but I like systems punters best.'

I've given away already the end of my story. After Melbourne Cup Day, we got stuck on a plateau for several months. We backed winners, but we backed even more losers, a few of them unplaced, which was doubly costly. The last Form-Plan horse that I backed ran at Flemington one wet day in the autumn of 1959. I forget its name but its colours were All brown and it was trained by one of the famous Hoysted family at Wangaratta. Its odds were eight-to-one, the longest I had ever been offered against a Form-Plan horse. If the horse had won, the system would have been in profit again, but the horse never flattered at any stage.

It would be easy to dismiss a betting method such as Form-Plan, and most of its disappointed followers surely did so. I would be fairly confident, though, that the average small punter who tries to back the winner of every race would be considerably better off at the end of each year after following Form-Plan or some similar method than after throwing his or her money at horse after horse in race after race. I even wish I had kept my old *Sporting Globe* collection for a few years afterwards and had checked the results of Form-Plan during the years after I had abandoned it. I don't recall when the ads for the system disappeared from the *Sporting Globe*, but I recall my receiving a newsletter from Mr Maclean at some time in 1959. He had decided to change some of the rules of his method. We were no longer to back horses starting from wide barriers or on days when the track was heavy. Needless to say, these rules would have prevented me from backing several losers during months past. The last message that I received from Mr Maclean was another newsletter. He had devised a completely new method of systematic betting. Results for the past few years were outstand-ing. Persons who had previously purchased Form-Plan could buy the new system at a discounted price. I decided that the man was incorrigible and a rogue, but that was a few years before I read Otto Fenichel's book. Now I incline to the belief that poor Mr Maclean was truly desperate to learn how he stood with God.

11. *Lickity and the Eccentric Aunt*

ONLY TWICE DURING my long lifetime have I intercepted from someone a look of admiration for my—what should I call it?—not wisdom but sagacity, perhaps, or shrewdness. And, strange to tell, I was grudgingly admired on both occasions on account of my involvement with Lickity (Cerise, gold hoops and cap).

I may have seemed ambivalent towards Teddy Ettershank in an earlier section, but the story of Lickity shows that Teddy sometimes took my father fully into his confidence, to their mutual advantage. Late in 1957, Teddy enlisted my father, and my father even enlisted me, in a carefully planned, massive, and ultimately successful off-course betting plunge.

Illegal off-course bookmakers operated in every suburb and town in Victoria for decades before the introduction of the TAB in 1961. At the Royal Commission that preceded the establishment of the TAB, one illegal bookmaker said in evidence that his annual turnover exceeded two million pounds. The report of the commission estimated that the total off-course turnover was at least three times the on-course turnover. And this was at a time when race meetings attracted crowds unheard of today. The off-course men were known as starting-price, or SP, bookmakers because they paid winning bets according to the odds on offer at the racecourse at the start of each race.

Teddy Ettershank and his mysterious band of followers mostly bet with on-course bookmakers. Teddy and two or three others would rush along the rails at an agreed time, calling out their bets to those leading bookmakers who knew them by name and with whom their credit was good. The aim was to get the best odds available before the weight of money obliged the bookmakers to reduce their odds. Sometimes, when they were betting with a very large sum, Teddy and his men might go along the rails a second time, but then, of course, they would have to accept lower odds and a lower overall return on their outlay.

Occasionally, Teddy would organise an off-course plunge. My guess is that he did this when the horse to be backed was considered a certainty and when the sum to be bet was huge, even by Teddy's standards. The advantage of an off-course plunge was that the money all went on at the best available odds. Moreover, if none of the smart men showed his face in the betting ring on course, let alone backed the horse in question with the bookmakers there, then the seeming lack of interest in the horse would cause on-course bookmakers to extend the horse's odds, thereby increasing the amount to be paid out by the off-course men. The only seeming drawback of an off-course plunge was its needing more men than usual to implement it—men whose credit was good with large off-course bookmakers and who could be trusted to phone their big bets through at the agreed time. This had to be just before the start of the race. (Sometimes a large SP operator was able to cover some of his risk by betting with a leading bookmaker on course. Employees of the biggest SP men went in and out of the turnstiles all day at the racecourse, phoning odds to their boss from nearby houses. Such men could be used to leak money back to the course, as the expression went, which reduced the starting price of the plunge-horse and hence the profit from the plunge.)

When Teddy was planning his off-course plunge on Lickity, I was working as a temporary clerk in the Bullion Office of the Royal Mint, in William Street, Melbourne. At the desk beside mine was Martin Dillon, who has been mentioned previously. I called him always *Mister* Dillon, but I'll call him here by his first name, given that I'm now nearly twenty years older than he was then. I was fascinated by Martin. There were probably thousands like him in Melbourne and in country Victoria, but I had led a sheltered life and he was the first of his kind that I had met. Martin had been brought up as a Catholic in Chiltern, in north-eastern Victoria, but had cheerfully given up his religion at an early age. I had heard of lapsed Catholics, as we called them in those days, but Martin was the first I had met. He and his wife had parted company many years before, and he'd had since then a number of what are nowadays called partners. In newspaper reports of the 1950s, they were called *de facto* wives or common-law wives, but Martin referred to them as his lady-friends.

I'd had a girlfriend for a few weeks soon after I began work at the Royal Mint, but for the rest of my time there I was a solitary, and my seeming content to remain so seemed to exasperate Martin. He tried to stir me to action with stories of his own youth. He made much use of the verb *to court*. At my age, in Chiltern, so he told me, he had courted never fewer than two girls at a time, and even in my innocence I understood that *to court* had for him a wider range of meaning than it had for me.

One day, I must have tried to explain to him that I had few opportunities to meet girls; that I had once gone alone on a Sunday picnic organised by the youth groups of my parish but had had to consort all day with solitary males like myself, while the young women were guarded by their boyfriends. Instead of answering me, he went into a sort of reverie, brought on, I supposed, by my mention of Catholic youth groups. He leaned back in his chair and said, more to himself than to me, that he had sometimes courted even Children of Mary, and his satisfaction seemed so genuine that I found myself believing his claim, scandalous though it seemed to me. (The Children of Mary was the title of a Catholic sodality, long since disappeared, whose members, all of them older girls or young women, attended mass together on a designated Sunday each month. In the great days of the sodality, a parish church might be more than half-filled with devout young female persons. I was intimidated even by the thought of such a gathering and kept well away from the church whenever the young females were assembled there but sometimes, on my way to a later mass, I saw a single Child of Mary or a small group going home through the quiet streets, each wearing the regalia of the sodality: a blue hood that reached below the waist and was topped by a sort of white veil, or so I seem to recall—I never got close enough to observe the details.)

When Martin Dillon wasn't trying to convert me to his way of life, we spent much of our time talking about racing. He went to every Saturday meeting and even took a day of his annual leave sometimes when he wanted to back a particular horse at a weekday meeting. On many a day while we were side by side at our desks, I would hear him phoning a bet to his SP bookmaker, whose name I still recall: Charlie Cotton. Martin knew a few small-time trainers and hard-bitten old stable hands and was sometimes tipped a winner. I resented his thinking I was no more than a mug punter and told him sometimes that my father knew some smart men around Flemington.

My father's SP bookmaker at that time was a man named Hughie Thomas. Hughie was no minnow as a bookmaker, and my father was prepared to phone to Hughie, five minutes before Lickity's race, a sizeable bet for Teddy and himself. On the evening before the race, my father gave me ten pounds (rather more than five hundred dollars in today's currency) and asked me to have Martin Dillon put the money on Lickity with his bookmaker. I was to pretend to Martin that an eccentric aunt of mine, who knew nothing about racing, had been tipped that the horse had a winning chance and had asked me to back it for her. I was not to hand over the money until ten minutes before the start of the race, as though the matter had slipped my mind until then.

All went as planned. Martin phoned my bet to Charlie Cotton, but he, Martin, reported to me with some surprise Charlie's telling him, when Lickity's name was mentioned, that a punter, only minutes before, had asked to have a huge amount on the horse. Charlie had had to limit the punter to a fraction of what he wanted to bet. When I heard this, I was surprised that Martin had not decided to have a small bet on Lickity for himself. Did he still believe my story about my aunt? Had it not yet occurred to him that the junior in the Bullion Office might, for once, be privy to valuable knowledge?

One last detail needs to be mentioned. The horses that Teddy and his men backed were mostly at short odds. The amount that they bet was such that a winner at three-to-one would give them an excellent result. Given that Teddy had told my father Lickity could not be beaten, we—my father and I—expected the horse to start at about two-to-one. The race was a good-quality maiden race at Warrnambool, and Lickity would have been about three-to-one in early betting. However, he was friendless in the ring, to use a racing expression. Not only did no big bettors want to back Lickity, but Teddy himself was at the meeting and made a great show of backing Lickity's nearest rival with several hundred pounds in cash. The laws of supply and demand operate unfailingly in the betting ring. Since no one seemed to want to back Lickity on course at Warrnambool, the bookmakers there lengthened his odds, hoping to tempt punters.

Meanwhile, all over Victoria and New South Wales, punters in the know were waiting to bet as much as their bookmakers would allow them on Lickity and, if the horse won, the bets were going to be paid at the odds being offered at Warrnambool when the race began.

Martin Dillon was always able to hear a broadcast of a weekday race if he was interested. A group of dedicated punters had a radio hidden somewhere in the Coining Hall or the Melting Department of the Mint. After he had backed Lickity for me, he went off to hear the race. I, being the boy around the place, stayed at my desk. When Martin came back, he seemed unusually thoughtful. He told me that my aunt must have got her tip from a reliable source, given that Lickity had led all the way and had won by four lengths.

A little later, out of curiosity, he phoned Charlie Cotton to see what the horse's odds had been. (So well organised were off-course bookmakers that their agents or spies on course could tell them the starting prices within minutes after each race.) I watched Martin while he asked Charlie what Lickity's odds had been. Martin would have expected, as I did, that the horse had started at around two- or three-to-one. He went on listening to Charlie the bookmaker for a minute or so, and I could see that even such a hardened old punter as Martin was hearing something that surprised him. He put the phone down and swung his chair around so that he faced me. He told me first that Lickity had started at five-to-one. Then he told me that Charlie had heard already on the grapevine that all the big SP bookmakers in Melbourne and Sydney had been taken by surprise and faced huge payouts. The plunge on Lickity had been one of the biggest and best-planned for years. And then I intercepted the first of the looks that I mentioned earlier.

I worked with Martin Dillon for only a few weeks after Lickity's win. In the new year, I left the Mint to begin a course at a primary teachers' college. During my last weeks with him, Martin seemed to have decided that I was not quite the girl-less, gormless teenager that he had taken me for. He even grinned at me sometimes and asked me to pass on to him any further tips that my aunt received.

Lickity had a short spell after his lucrative win and did not race again until the autumn of 1958. His next start was to be at Bendigo, in a stronger field than he had beaten at Warrnambool. This time there would be no huge plunge, but Teddy had told my father to back the horse with confidence. I told my father I could easily take a day's sick leave from the teachers' college, and he entrusted me with twenty pounds. My father sometimes exhibited a mild paranoia in racing matters. He warned me to stay well away from the rails bookmakers where Teddy and his men would be betting. Teddy had not set eyes on me since I was a boy of ten, but my father was afraid that Teddy might recognise me and might be annoyed if I seemed to be putting mine and my father's money on before the smart men had got theirs on.

I travelled to Bendigo on one of the buses that for many years took racegoers to country meetings from opposite Ball and Welch's store in Flinders Street. Most of the passengers were elderly, but the man who sat beside me and began a conversation was in his late twenties. He was good company, and we talked for most of the trip. He was an accountant from Wollongong, a bachelor taking his annual holidays alone but on public transport in order to meet people. He was going to the races but was going to stay in Bendigo for a few days to see the sights, as he put it. I told him that I had lived in Bendigo as a small boy, which was true, and that I was hoping to meet up at the races with family and friends from former times. This was not at all true. I had no relatives in Bendigo and had lost all contact with former friends. The only persons who might have been pleased to meet me at the races were the Bourke brothers. They were licensed bookmakers and also SP men. When my father had taken us away in haste from Bendigo ten years before, he had owed the Bourke brothers a huge amount. Perhaps they could have taken me hostage and sent a ransom note to my father. I am only joking—but when I did see one of the Bourke men in the distance later that day, I turned away at once. I could not have dared to look him in the eye.

The accountant and I did not stay together at the races, although we watched a few races from the same vantage point. I told him nothing about Lickity. My responsibility was to get my bet on quietly at the back of the ring and, if all went well, to collect my winnings quietly afterwards. There was no saying what the man from Wollongong might have done if I had told him to have a modest bet on Lickity. I thought of accountants as wealthy men. For all I knew, he might have had a roll of notes on him and might have launched a plunge of his own.

Lickity was again at generous odds, perhaps because his opposition was stronger. His opening odds were three-to-one, but these soon lengthened. I added five pounds of my own to my father's twenty. I found a man betting four-to-one in the back row and backed Lickity to win a hundred pounds. I kept away from the accountant and watched the race alone. Lickity led all the way and won almost as easily as he had won at Warrnambool.

I had obeyed my father's instructions and had kept away from the rails bookmakers, but my betting with a man at the rear of the ring had the disadvantage that I had to collect my winnings in view of the crowd passing to and fro on the main lawn. I had collected my bundle of notes and was folding them into my pocket when I saw the accountant watching me from a distance. Another sort of man might not have felt obliged to say anything, but I have always tried to cover my embarrassment by talking. I walked over to the man and began to tell him about my eccentric aunt. I had met her before the last race…She didn't like betting with bookmakers and had asked me to bet for her…The more I talked, the more foolish I sounded, but the man from Wollongong was too polite to challenge my story. He was, it seemed, rather impressed, for he gave me the second of the two looks mentioned earlier.

12. *Orange, Purple Sleeves, Black Cap*

MANY YEARS HAVE passed since I gave up watching films. Even as a young man, I was beginning to tire of their complicated plots, their too-clever dialogue, and the soulful stares of the leading actors. On a certain rainy afternoon in the late 1950s, however, I travelled alone on a suburban train into central Melbourne to watch an English film called *The Rainbow Jacket*. The plot was improbable, to say the least, and the acting was unconvincing, but I considered my long trip worthwhile. A few days before, I had read, in a lukewarm review, that the film, which was in Technicolor, included footage of actual races on English racecourses. As it turned out, the actual scenes lasted only a few minutes but I got from them what I had hoped to get: I had seen for the first time the details of a few sets of the racing colours of England. The appearance on the screen of each set of colours was so brief that I could recall afterwards not one complete design. I remembered only glimpses of details: a cap with hoops of bottle-green and lilac, perhaps, or the striking X-shape on a primrose or canary ground of chocolate-brown crossed sashes, as I would have called them, although the English call them, so I learned much later, cross belts. I recalled only a jumble of such details but they confirmed what I had suspected since I had begun to study racing colours ten years before: that Australian colours were generally dull and predictable, whereas English colours, even allowing for their being unfamiliar to me, had an extraordinary variety and were, in general, more distinctive or assertive than those worn in Australia. That word *assertive* may seem odd in its context, but I'll explain later my use of it.

Perhaps twenty-five years after I had watched *The Rainbow Jacket*, I was loitering in High Street, Armadale, one of the fashionable shopping precincts in Melbourne's inner south-east, while my wife was looking through clothing stores. We had not been to Armadale for several years, and I was wondering whether I might find a bookshop among the upmarket shopfronts. In the arcade near the railway station I found not just a bookshop but one dedicated to books and prints with horses as their subject matter. I went inside, walked past the many shelves of books about show horses, equestrian events, that sort of thing, and found the horse-racing section. The proprietor, or whoever he was, asked if I was looking for anything in particular. This sort of question usually irritates me, but something about the man prompted me to confide in him. It's a lonely life sometimes, being obsessed with horse racing and having no one to share your obsession with, and I was hoping, perhaps, that the man had read some of the books he dealt in and had been affected by them. I told him I had a fair-sized horse-racing library at home but that it had always lacked a certain sort of book—a book that probably didn't exist, even though I often dreamed about it. Yes, I told the man, I had this dream that I would one day walk into an unfamiliar bookshop and would find on an obscure shelf a massive volume containing illustrations of thousands of sets of racing colours, preferably but not necessarily from England. The man, so it turned out, had a liking for the dramatic. While I was talking, he did a sort of sideways shuffle towards me. Still looking attentively into my face, he reached a hand up to a shelf behind my head. When I had finished speaking, he held out for my inspection a heavy volume of about A4 size with a plain-looking dark-green cover. He asked me off-handedly whether this was the sort of book I had in mind.

The book is beside me now, as I write. I paid fifty dollars for it in the early 1980s. If the price had been a thousand dollars, I would have put it on layby and would have bought no other books until I had saved up for it. The title is *The Benson and Hedges Book of Racing Colours*, and the publisher is the Jockeys' Association of Great Britain. The book was published in 1973. The story behind its publication is told in the preliminary pages. It seems the Jockeys' Association came up with the idea as a fundraiser for their Injured Jockeys' Fund. The makers of Benson and Hedges cigarettes paid for production costs. The owners of more than nine thousand registered sets of racing colours gave permission for their colours to be reproduced in the book. How many copies were sold or how much money went towards helping injured jockeys I'll never know. Nor will the persons who brought the book into being ever know how much satisfaction I've derived from it.

The book fell open just now at pages ninety-four and ninety-five. Fifty-six sets of colours are arranged before me. Among them are those of Mr P. C. Evans: Mauve and pink chevrons, mauve cap. I learn from the opposite page that Lord Fairhaven's colours are Copper, silver hoop, armlets and cap. I'll try another page...I learn from page 236 that Capt. C. R. Radclyffe's colours are Dark blue, grey sash, collar, cuffs and cap, while Mr Mohammad Rafique's colours are Black, old-gold sash, sleeves and hooped cap. So what? the reader may be asking. Why should it matter that someone in England forty years ago chose this or that design for his or her colours?

There are people, so I've read, for whom numerals or letters of the alphabet have each a different colour. In *Remembrance of Things Past*, by Marcel Proust, the narrator associates the vowel sounds in certain place names with distinctive colours or shades. I am someone for whom each shade or colour has a rudimentary quality of the sort attributed to persons, while combinations of colours bring me hints of personalities. Surely many people are as fascinated by colour as I am—if not by racing colours. I suspect my interest in colour is linked to my having no sense of smell. I have trouble sometimes convincing people of this, but I have never smelled any sort of odour. I have held under my nose flowers said to be rich in fragrance and detected nothing. I once sat calmly reading in a room that was filling with gas after my saucepan had boiled over and had put out the flame on my stove. When I hear or read about odours, I see in my mind colours. The odour of a red rose is red; the smell of gas is a bright blue. I

used the word *assertive* in an earlier paragraph. For me, each colour
or combination of colours asserts something. To put it simply: for as
long as I can remember, I've believed that colours are trying to tell
me something.

Racing colours for me are not unlike national flags or heraldic
coats of arms. The colours of many a flag are intended to suggest
the hopes or beliefs of the nation it represents or, sometimes,
landscapes or waterways. Likewise, coats of arms often speak of
the history or of the achievements of their bearers. My interpreta-
tions of racing colours might seem arbitrary or fanciful to many
but they have their own consistency—while my beliefs about
colour have grown more complicated over time, the basics were
established during my childhood.

The first colours that I saw were those of the trainer of harness
horses Clarry Long, who was mentioned, along with his colours,
in an earlier section. The first set that I handled were those carried
by a horse named Zimmy that my father owned and trained for
a few months in Bendigo, in the mid-1940s. My father, who was
mostly short of money, had scrounged the colours from someone
who no longer needed them and had registered them in his own
name. They appeared in race books as Yellow, purple armbands and
cap, but according to my strict rules in these matters they should
have been described as Yellow, violet hooped sleeves and cap. I
enjoyed the feel of the fabric and I admired the way it was stretched
over the buttons on the jacket, but I was less attracted to the colours
and design than I had been to Clarry Long's brown with pale-blue
stars and, although I have no memory of it, I feel sure that I must
have used my school pastels sometimes to design jackets and caps of

various arrangements of brown and pale blue, wondering as I did so why the two colours together affected me as they did.

The first illustration of racing colours that I saw was on a small glossy poster that fell out from between the pages of the *Leader*, a long-defunct weekly magazine produced by the publishers of the *Age* as a rival to the *Weekly Times*. The poster celebrated the achievements of Bernborough and showed the big bay horse with jockey up and wearing the colours of Azzalin Romano, who owned Bernborough late in his career. This was perhaps the first of many instances in my life when I've been much more affected by an illustration of something or a written account of something than by the thing itself. This was in the 1940s, when coloured illustrations often seemed more like paintings than reproductions of photographs, and the rich tints of the poster affected me much more than had the sight of Clarry Long's jacket or the feel of Zimmy's yellow and violet.

Mr Romano's colours were Orange, purple sleeves, black cap. Now, even though Bernborough is my all-time-favourite horse, I maintain that I would have been drawn to the orange and purple and black no matter what horse had carried them. Many years after both Bernborough and Mr Romano were dead, the colours were re-registered in the name of Sir Tristan Antico, like Romano a successful businessman of Italian descent. Sir Tristan owned some very good horses but many moderate performers also. Almost every week at the races I saw his colours going around, as they say, and I never failed to admire them and to feel again some of the attraction that they had for me long before. Part of the attraction comes from the simple tripartite design. There are no spots or checks or diamonds clamouring for attention—only three zones of uniform colour, each quietly influencing the appeal of the other. At the risk of baffling, or even amusing, some readers, I will try to put into words my reaction to the colours. I associate the orange and the purple and the black with quiet confidence, with dignity, and with unshakeable resolve.

Only one other set of colours has affected me in somewhat the way that I've been trying to describe. I never actually saw the colours; I only read them from a race book. In the 1950s, when most colours in Victoria were dull and predictable, a horse named Nitro was entered at a meeting that I attended at Warrnambool. The horse was scratched from its race, and I don't recall hearing of it again or of any other horse with the same colours. I owned a set of coloured pencils by then and used them often to illustrate Nitro's colours and to ponder over them and delight in them: Grey, orange sleeves, red armbands and cap.

Nitro's were far from being the only colours that I illustrated with coloured pencils. All through the 1950s, and at intervals since, I've felt a need to produce coloured miniatures of actual sets of colours that I've seen or read about or of sets that I myself have designed. In the early years, I had no other motive than to see in front of me and to enjoy the immense variety of racing colours, whether actual or imagined. In time, however, I understood that I was engaged in a serious task: I was searching for my ideal colours, for the unique combination that could represent me to the world. I've preserved most of the many hundreds of colours that I tried on, as you might say. In early years, I strove to be original. Many of my designs used diagonal stripes, which were extremely rare but later became almost fashionable. If Pablo Picasso went through a Blue period, I once went through a green-and-blue period. Like diagonal stripes, green and blue were rarely seen together although, like diagonal stripes, they later became widely used. In fact, I would have gone through many more periods than did Picasso before I settled, nearly thirty years ago, on the combination of brown and lilac. Those are my colours to this day, but I have never yet settled on a satisfactory design.

I described the task as serious, and I do take it seriously. I've devoted myself to horse racing as other sorts of person devote themselves to religious or political or cultural enterprises, although I hope I can still make a joke at my own expense. I read once that certain musical compositions (by Bach? by Beethoven? I forget) sounded like the efforts of the human soul to explain itself to God. If ever I find my perfect combination of brown and lilac, I'll feel as though I've thus explained myself. But I seem destined never to find my perfect set of colours. Is this because I've deluded myself for most of my life? Are racing colours not half so eloquent as I've always believed? Or, is my soul too much of a mess for explanation?

13. *Pavia and Tulloch*

ACCORDING TO MY fifty-years-old *Times Atlas of the World*, Pavia is a town or city about forty kilometres south of Milan. The same name, Pavia, belongs also to a dot on the map about ninety kilometres east of Lisbon. However, when a man named Jack Casamento calls one of his horses Pavia we can surely assume that he wants to commemorate the Italian rather than the Portuguese place.

Pavia (Dark-blue-and-pink diagonal stripes) first came to my notice when he won a restricted race at a summer meeting at Warrnambool in the late 1950s. The horse's form before the race had been moderate, and he had started at about twelve-to-one. About twenty minutes after the race, when the placegetters and the also-rans had all been returned to their stalls, I saw a swarthy grey-haired man collecting a wad of ten-pound notes from a rails bookmaker. I followed the man and saw him collect a similar wad from each of two other bookmakers, and I had no doubt that I was watching the owner-trainer of Pavia. I've always enjoyed whatever glimpses I could get of the ways of racing folk, and so I followed Jack Casamento and watched from afar while he and a stable hand rubbed down the horse Pavia, packed up their gear, and then led the horse out towards the car park. Jack's natural expression seemed to be a scowl, and I decided he would have been a tough man to deal with, both on and off the racecourse.

My father's younger brother Louis, who was mentioned in an earlier section, lived in or near Warrnambool all his life. I learned from him later that day that Jack Casamento had made his money as a wholesale dealer in fruit and vegetables. Several times weekly, he bought a truckload of greengroceries at the big wholesale market in Melbourne, drove the stuff to Warrnambool, and then sold it there to greengrocers and mixed businesses. Louis then announced two other interesting things about the owner-trainer of Pavia.

The previous sentence is not quite accurate. I had arrived at the races that day with Louis and a man named Joe Rowan, who was a distant cousin of Louis and my father and was on holiday from Sydney. Joe was a married man of about forty years; Louis was about the same age but a bachelor. I was an innocent young man in his late teens. When Louis had explained how Jack Casamento earned his livelihood, he, Louis, had addressed his remarks equally to me and to Joe Rowan. But then, when Louis had reported the next interesting item about the owner-trainer of Pavia, he, Louis, had looked only at Joe and had lowered his voice as though he wanted me not to hear him, although he surely knew that I heard every word. What Louis muttered was that Jack Casamento kept a harem. I would have been too embarrassed to ask what exactly Louis meant, but Joe asked him at once. Louis explained himself, still looking only at Joe and still as though I was not meant to hear. I was surprised to hear my puritanical bachelor-uncle use an expression that I had heard only among my peers. Jack Casamento, so Louis said, lived with a mother and a daughter and was *on* with both women.

When I'm watching a race that I've bet on, I naturally will my own horse to win, although I mostly follow my father's example and never utter a word or a cry during the running of the race. When I'm watching a race without having had a bet, I'm never equanimical or neutral. I'm always anxious on behalf of one or, sometimes, two or three horses owned or trained or ridden by persons for whom I feel an affinity. I've never owned the least share in a racehorse or known more than a handful of racehorse owners. For nearly thirty years, however, I taught general education and public speaking at the School for Apprentice Jockeys that was formerly conducted by the Victoria Racing Club and supervised by members of the panel of stipendiary stewards. During that time, I dealt with dozens of young persons who were later successful jockeys. A few are still riding today. Some are now trainers. I dealt to a lesser extent with the apprentices' masters, the trainers, who were, some of them, prosperous and successful while others seemed to live from hand to mouth. Some of the trainers that I once met are still training today. I've had no official connection with racing for more than twenty years, but I still get pleasure today from the success of a jockey or a trainer that I was on good

terms with many years ago. Even so, most of the jockeys and trainers that I wish well or barrack for are total strangers to me. Well,
that may be true for the big names of racing, so to call them, whose
faces I see only in newspaper illustrations or through my binoculars when I train them on the distant mounting yard at some city
meeting. At country meetings, spectators can get close enough to
the main actors to hear their every word. At a non-TAB meeting
in the remote district where I live nowadays, I can often hear every
word of the instructions from a trainer to a jockey before a race
and every word of a report from a jockey to a trainer after a race.
In short, even though I've been for much of my life a mere specta-
tor at the races, I've dealt enough with racing people or I've spied
enough on them to enable me to form preferences: to watch races
hoping that my favourite persons succeed.

When I had first seen the stern-faced owner-trainer of Pavia
collecting his wads of notes from the bookmakers, I had felt drawn
to him at once. I was ready to welcome him into the company of
those whose fortunes I followed week after week and year after
year in the form guides and results pages of newspapers. I foresaw
myself looking in future for the names Pavia or Casamento in the
back pages of newspapers and mentally urging on the dark blue
and the pink, and the tough-looking man whose colours they were.
My uncle's telling me that Jack had become prosperous as a wholesale merchant would only have increased my liking for him. He
was no inheritor of wealth but someone who had worked for it.
He was at the fruit and vegetable market in Footscray before dawn
several days each week. He drove backwards and forwards along
the Princes Highway during week after week for year after year.

And he knew how to prepare a horse to win at double-figure odds. Go, Jack!

But what was I to make of the keeper of the harem? Should I be investing emotional capital in such a man? Aligning myself with the dark blue and pink, and urging home a horse owned and trained by a public sinner? I can't say that these questions cost me any sleep at the time, but I do remember asking them of myself. My answers would have differed from month to month, even from week to week. My moral compass swung often and wildly during that period of my life. This was not only because I was going through a process that my devout uncle Louis would have called *losing the faith* if only he had known about it. If, as a believing Catholic, I considered the keeping of a harem a breach of the Commandments and a mortal sin, then I could hardly wish for a harem-keeper a successful career on the turf. On the other hand, even during those periods when I considered myself a freethinker or an agnostic or whatever, I found the notion of a mother-and-daughter harem distasteful or even repugnant. My own instinct was to respect or even to fear females. I was not so much inclined to condemn Jack the harem-keeper. Rather, I could not understand what seemed to me his barbarous way of life; I thought his view of the world must be utterly remote from my own.

The second of the other two interesting things that Louis told to Joe Rowan and me was an account of how Jack Casamento had come to be the owner-trainer of Pavia. Louis had heard the story from one of Jack's acquaintances and said he had no reason to doubt that it was essentially true.

Until 1956, the few horses that Jack Casamento had owned and trained had been bought cheaply from small-time owners or trainers like himself. Early in 1956, Jack decided on a new and bold policy. His business had prospered, and he planned to buy a well-bred yearling at the autumn sales. He might have chosen his yearling at the sales in Melbourne or Adelaide, but he was even more ambitious. He obtained a catalogue from the famous Trentham sales, in Wellington, New Zealand, and set about drawing up a short list of possible purchases. His price limit was a thousand guineas or thereabouts. (A guinea was twenty-one shillings or one pound and one shilling. As a unit of currency it was no longer used except at horse sales. I believe the custom was for the company in charge of the sale to take a shilling from each guinea as commission. This would have equalled 4.76 per cent of the sale price.) A thousand guineas was by no means a trifling sum—the average race at a Melbourne meeting in the late 1950s had total prize money of a thousand pounds. Jack studied the catalogue long and hard, so the story went, and compiled his short list. Equal at the top were two colts by the sire Khorassan. One was from a mare named Royal Battle; the dam of the other was named Florida.

The next part of the story had several variations. Depending on who told the story, Jack chose his purchase after looking at the colts themselves, or he decided to let the colt from Florida pass because bidders were few and he supposed he might have overlooked some fault that other buyers had noticed in the animal. Perhaps Jack himself was unable to recall afterwards exactly why he bought the Royal Battle colt for a thousand guineas while the Sydney trainer Tommy Smith bought the Florida colt for seven hundred and fifty. Certainly, Jack would have had no cause to reflect on the reasons for his purchase until at least six months after the sales, when the colt that Jack named Pavia was being prepared for racing and when the colt that had been named Tulloch had won, at Randwick in early October 1956, the first of the thirty-six races that he would win during his illustrious career.

I suppose sometimes that I should have felt an overwhelming pity for Jack Casamento after learning how close he had come to selecting the horse I rank second only to Bernborough from those that have raced during my lifetime. I felt instead a sort of annoyance. How could a shrewd horseman sift through a thick sales catalogue and come within a whisker of choosing a future champion of champions, only to fumble at the last moment? Or was I secretly supposing that God had found a subtle but agonising means of punishing for the rest of his life the keeper of a harem?

I could never forget Tulloch's career, but I've forgotten what became of Pavia after the day when I first saw him win at Warrnambool. I have a vague recollection of his winning a few restricted races in later years. I clearly recall seeing him carry the dark blue and pink in a steeplechase at Flemington towards the end of his career. I'm not sure that he wasn't killed in a jumping race or put down after being severely injured. If that happened, then I would have felt only sympathy for Jack Casamento.

It seems unthinkable now that anyone but the master-trainer Tommy Smith should have had Tulloch in his stable, but I sometimes tried to get my uncle Louis speculating on the subject of what would have happened to Tulloch if he had begun his career with the name Pavia and in the care of Jack Casamento at Warrnambool. Louis had only one answer. 'Jack would have poisoned him.' Louis meant, of course, not that Jack would have intentionally done away with the potential champion but that, in his eagerness to make a good thing of Tulloch alias Pavia, he would have ruined the horse's health with immoderate dosages of what are called nowadays performance-enhancing substances.

14. *Basil Burgess at Moonee Valley*

ONE OF THE many colloquial expressions that I enjoy hearing or using is the description of some or another man as having short arms and deep pockets, meaning that he pays for his shout or buys a raffle ticket reluctantly, if at all. I've always considered myself a prompt payer and generous with money, and perhaps I am, but I learned at several racecourses during the last months of 1974 that I'm a punter with short arms and deep pockets.

In the early months of 1974, my salary was higher than ever before and higher than it would be until nearly twenty years later, when the college of advanced education where I then worked became part of a university and I became a senior lecturer. In early 1974, I was the assistant editor in the Publications Branch of the Education Department of Victoria. I was second in charge of a staff of about twenty and could expect to become editor in five or ten years, depending on when my boss chose to retire. The work was pleasant enough, but my heart was not in it. Telling twenty people what to do and trying to keep up with my boss, who was driven by a manic energy, left me in no mood to write fiction during my evenings and weekends. I had been writing fiction in my free time for nearly ten years. My first book was on its way to being published, and I had begun a second, but I could not foresee myself keeping up my double life for much longer.

An unlikely solution suggested itself. House husbands, as they later came to be called, were unheard of at that time, but my wife and I decided that I should become one. We were not trying to bring in a new social order; we simply did what suited us both, even though our household income was somewhat reduced. My wife had been confined to the house with our three small sons for four years and wanted to resume her career. I was used to helping with housework and shopping and child minding, and I looked forward to spending the day in a quiet house instead of a stressful office. The new set-up worked well for a few years, until our sons' upbringing began to cost more than my wife's income alone could provide, but that's another story.

I knew better than to expect much money from the sales of my books of literary fiction, but I hoped to earn a modest income from betting—yes, betting on racehorses. Despite my father's dismal record and my own lack of success in earlier years, I still believed I could beat the odds. I had a new approach to punting. Since I had started to bet, in the year after I left school, I had gone to each race meeting with a small sum, hoping to turn it into a large sum.

My new approach, in the 1970s, seemed much more businesslike. I would set myself up with a comparatively large betting bank; I would have a few large bets each day; I would expect a profit of only twenty per cent of my turnover. And where was the comparatively large bank to come from? Well, superannuation in those days was not as regulated as it has since become. I had been on the payroll of the Education Department for nearly fifteen years, first as a primary teacher and then as a publications officer, and had had deducted from my salary the maximum permissible amount of contributions to the defined-benefits superannuation scheme of the state government. On my resignation, I would have all my contributions returned to me—not rolled over but paid to me in cash, no questions asked. My wife's father had escaped the Great Depression by finding employment with the Department of Agriculture as a stock inspector and had more reverence for superannuation than the ancient Israelites could have had for manna. If he had learned that I was cashing in my superannuation to use as a racing bank, he would have horsewhipped me. I forget how we kept him from finding out. I was paying for some large life-insurance policies at the time, and we may have lied to him that I used my super to buy more such policies. Anyway, when the Education Department had paid up, there I was with perhaps twenty-five thousand dollars in today's money for use as my racing bank.

I divided the money theoretically into a hundred betting units. I planned to have five bets at each meeting that I attended. I would watch the bookmakers' boards and would back well-supported horses or shorteners, as they were called, at average odds of about five-to-one. I would count on one of my five horses winning, which would return to me a profit of one unit per meeting. I hoped to attend about eighty meetings each year—most of them metropolitan meetings but a few at nearer country courses. (One of our neighbours, a young mother herself, was eager to be paid for minding my sons when I went to the occasional country meeting.) If my estimations were correct, I would earn each year about eighty betting units, or about eighty per cent of my bank. This would be a useful addition to my wife's salary. She, by the way, had no objection to my scheme. I was not even required to explain it to her. She was a spendthrift with no patience for budgets or any sort of investments. She also trusted me. I'd had only trifling bets for as long as we had been together and had managed the family finances prudently. Unlike her father, she hardly understood what a superannuation scheme was.

The first two meetings of my new career were at city courses. I felt reluctant to rush into betting. Instead, I told myself I would bet in only small amounts as a sort of warm-up or induction program. On each day I backed my hoped-for winner and made a minuscule profit on my small bets. I still felt no eagerness to bet on my intended scale, but I no longer had any excuse for delaying my career as a professional or, at least, a semi-professional punter.

The next meeting was at Werribee, only a short train trip from Melbourne. Werribee was more a country town than a suburb then, and the race trains used to stop at a special platform beside the course. I strode from the racecourse platform towards the betting ring with a hundred dollars in what I thought of as my racing pocket. Each of my five bets would be twenty dollars straight out, that is, win-only.

The first two horses that I selected and backed were beaten— one thoroughly but the other only narrowly. I had lost forty dollars, or about five hundred in today's currency. Having a large bank is meant to keep a punter calm during losing runs of ten or twelve. I had backed only two losers but I was by no means calm. I let two races pass, telling myself the betting gave me no clear indication. Before the following race, one horse was clearly being backed by men in the know. Its odds shortened from eights to fives or sixes. This was the horse that I had to back.

I have never been able to recall the horse's name. I recall that it was trained at the old Epsom course in Mordialloc and that the rider wore mostly black with markings of green and yellow. My not recalling the name tells me that I must have been under considerable strain at the time. I won't try to describe how I dithered and hesitated or how I went past one after another bookmaker with my twenty-dollar note in my hand until something caused me to push my way out of the betting ring and to go to the totalisator and bet five dollars win-only on the shortener, which, of course, won with ease.

I had no more bets that day. I had to stay until the last race because my only means of getting home was by race train. If the meeting had been in Melbourne, I would have gone home at once by train or tram. I was neither angry nor upset. I was bemused by what I had learned about myself that day. Unlike my father, who seemed to lose all sense of the value of money when a race was in the offing, I seemed to have a built-in regulator that would not allow me to bet more than a certain amount. I might have said that whenever I stepped onto a racecourse my arms became short and my pockets deep.

What surprises me nowadays is that I had not already learned my limitations as a punter nearly fifteen years before, on the day when Basil Burgess brought his two horses, On Parade and Agathis (both carrying Red, royal-blue sash) to a meeting at Moonee Valley. Many New Zealanders brought their horses each year to Melbourne for the spring carnival, but Basil Burgess had crossed the Tasman in midwinter and each of his two horses was entered in a minor race.

The New Zealanders fascinated me—the owners and trainers, I mean. For one thing, their country had legislated bookmakers out of existence decades before. The only legal form of betting was with the totalisator. To launch in New Zealand the sort of betting plunges that took place in Australia would have been counterproductive— the greater the sum invested, the less the win dividend. How, I often wondered, did the many smart men in New Zealand profit from their smartness or their inside information? I supposed that their policy must have been secrecy at all costs; that knowledge of a horse's prospects must have been shared among the fewest possible people; that a stable's commission was launched not by three or four well- known identities in full view of other punters but by one person alone—perhaps someone's nonchalant-looking wife or mother-in- law—with instructions to wait until three minutes before the race before discreetly handing over a bundle of notes at a tote window.

Whether or not as a result of their having only the tote to bet with, the New Zealanders seemed to me even less predictable than the shrewdest of their Australian counterparts. I recall an example of New Zealand acumen at work. At a Caulfield meeting not long before the Cup itself, a New Zealand trainer had two horses engaged. When interviewed by a racing journalist on the Friday, the trainer talked up the chances of one of the horses, which was a leading contender for the Caulfield Cup. The other horse was not mentioned in the interview. Even if the journalist had asked about the horse, the trainer must have claimed it was not worth writing about. On the Saturday, the Caulfield Cup hope ran fourth at short odds. The other horse, named either Cybeau or Sybeau, and carrying dark-green-and-white stripes, ran in a minor race on the program. The horse was leading the field by three lengths when they passed me in the old Guineas stand and was even further in front at the post. It had been friendless in the betting, as the saying goes, and had started at forty-to-one.

On the evening before the meeting at Moonee Valley, I spent much time and effort in trying to anticipate Basil Burgess's moves. I was convinced that one of his horses would win or go close to winning while the other would be saved for another day. On Parade was third- or fourth-favourite in an early race on the program while Agathis, which had very poor form, was an outsider in a later race. I had such an exaggerated opinion of the cunning of men such as Burgess that I arrived at the course almost persuaded not to back On Parade and to have two pounds—my standard bet at the time—on the unfancied Agathis. I might have followed this extreme course of action, except that On Parade seemed unwanted in the betting before the race. I could not resist the ten-to-one on offer and had what I would have considered a half-bet on the horse: ten-pounds-to-one, win-only. On Parade won easily.

As the time for Agathis's race drew near, my thinking was tangled indeed. I was trying, or so I thought, to outguess a man who made a living, or so I thought, from conduct that was unguessable. The most obvious possibility seemed to be that Basil Burgess had achieved his goal for the day and that Agathis would finish in the ruck and would be worth backing at a later date. But I began to question this line of thinking about fifteen minutes before Agathis's race when Frank McCann, easily the biggest bookmaker in the old South Hill enclosure, was betting thirty-three-to-one against the horse. These were lucrative odds for a horse trained by a cunning New Zealander. I began to consider the possibility that Basil Burgess was putting into practice that day what I have since heard described as reverse psychology. What if the New Zealander was demonstrating his cunningness by behaving without any seeming cunningness? What if suspicious punters such as myself were tying themselves in mental knots in an effort to anticipate Burgess's plans while he himself was behaving with transparent honesty? In short, I came around to the conclusion that Agathis was worth backing.

If I'd had the courage of my convictions—if I had dared to back my assessment of the deviousness of Basil and his fellow countrymen, then I should have bet all my winnings from On Parade on the stablemate in the hope of winning more than three hundred pounds, which would have been a small fortune for me. The thought of risking my ten pounds, however, caused me to question my own judgement about the degree of Basil Burgess's cunningness. My doubts multiplied as the time for the race approached. Before I left the ring, I had half a pound, or ten shillings, on Agathis at thirty-three-to-one. The other nine and a half pounds of my winnings stayed at the bottom of one of my deep pockets and well out of reach of my short arms while Agathis completed a winning double for owner-trainer Basil Burgess at Moonee Valley.

15. *P. S. Grimwade in the Central Highlands*

I'VE MENTIONED THAT racing is for me what religion is for another sort of person, and that this is a serious matter. Racing provides me with a set of beliefs and a way of life. Racing also, like many a religion, has its saints. These are, for me anyway, legendary rather than historical figures. The legends surrounding the saints are all of my own making. This could hardly be otherwise, given that mine is largely a one-man religion with myself as bishop, priest, congregation and, in this instance, hagiographer.

In the years when I was mastering the art of reading, we had few books in our house but I got plenty of practice with headlines in newspapers, captions on advertisements, word balloons in cartoons and comic strips, and labels on packets, cans, and bottles. I don't know why my father kept a bottle of hydrogen peroxide in the bathroom. Did he clean his teeth with the stuff? Put drops of it into his ears to dislodge wax? Anyway, I saw the bottle often. The glass was brown. The label had a border of green and was dense with black words on a white ground. I would have read the words often, although many were surely beyond my comprehension. I remember three today: the three surnames comprising the business name of the company that had bottled the stuff. The three were Felton, Grimwade, and Guerin.

I don't recall having seen the name Guerin in any context since I read it on the label of the bottle nearly seventy years ago. (After I had written that statement, I looked into a Melbourne phone directory from ten years ago and found about forty subscribers with that surname!) When I was first taken to the art gallery, as we called it when it was housed long ago in part of the building now given over to the State Library, I saw the words *Felton Bequest* displayed beside many a painting, although I did not learn until many years later that one of the family of the bottlers of patent medicines had left an immense sum to the gallery. If I had read the business pages or the society pages of newspapers when I was young, I would surely have seen the name Grimwade from time to time. I was never a reader of those pages, and yet, when I first saw the name in a race book in the late 1950s, I had somehow learned that bearers of that uncommon name were likely to be company directors from Toorak or nearby suburbs and direct or indirect beneficiaries of a fortune mostly accumulated during the nineteenth century.

I know few facts about Mr P. S. Grimwade, but I recall the day when I first backed one of his racehorses. It was early spring in 1957, and racing was at Moonee Valley. A few days before the Moonee

Valley meeting, I had heard from Martin Dillon, my colleague at the Royal Mint, that a horse named Sanvo (colours will be provided later) was surely being set to win a city race at long odds. Martin had noticed Sanvo at several recent country meetings. The three-years-old had been at comparatively short odds but had run poorly and had been *dead* in the sense of the word that Martin and I understood.

This is the place for me to report about Martin the belief or doctrine of his that most earned my admiration. My father, Teddy Ettershank, and most other punters that I knew or knew of reserved their biggest bets for favourites or horses at short odds. If they backed a horse at long odds, which they did only rarely, they outlaid only a fraction of what they would have bet if the horse had been at short odds. Martin Dillon was fond of saying that if he fancied a horse at long odds he would put *much more* on the horse than his usual stake. Martin liked to appear a man of quirks and eccentricities, but his fondness for long odds was genuine. I was with him in the paddock enclosure at Caulfield on Memsie Stakes Day in 1957 when a man with stable information told him that Gay Saba (Black-and-white stripes, red sash, sleeves and cap) was going to be well backed to win a sprint race.

Gay Saba was a middle-distance horse returning from a spell, and I was reluctant to back him, but Martin Dillon had fifteen pounds on the horse at twenty-to-one, after which I had my own modest bet. Martin even coupled Gay Saba in doubles with the favoured few horses in the race following. Gay Saba duly won, as did one of the favourites in the later race. I won modestly and Martin collected the equivalent of about twenty thousand dollars in today's currency. His colleagues had often told me of Martin's achievement with the horse Lucky Stride (Brown-and-white quarters) in the Oakleigh Plate of 1956, which was the year before I went to work at the Mint. Lucky Stride, which came from New South Wales, had finished only midfield in the previous Oakleigh Plate, in 1955, but Martin maintained that it might have won if it had not been badly checked in the straight. Before the 1956 Plate, he told anyone who would listen that the horse would win and that he was going to have twenty pounds on it. Lucky Stride won, and Martin got forty-to-one for his money.

When Martin had first told me about Sanvo's being set for a city race, he was hoping to back it at twenty-to-one or more, but no more than ten-to-one was bet against it at Moonee Valley. Martin and I were in different enclosures that day, but he told me later that he'd had a big bet on the horse. For once, I had a big bet myself, according to my own scale of betting. Everything that Martin had predicted proved accurate, except that the horse dead-heated for first and we collected only half our anticipated winnings.

That was the day when I first had the opportunity to study the Grimwade racing colours and to infer from them that the man they represented was thoughtful, discriminating, and with a preference for the uncommon and the subtle. The colours seemed simple at first sight: Green-and-white hoops, blue cap. Unlike most sets of colours, however, which I took in at a glance, these provoked me to ponder on them; to call them up again and again in my mind; to try to analyse their effect on me. Green and white was by no means an uncommon combination in Victoria in the 1950s. The Steele family, who had made their fortune from retailing furniture, had the colours Green, white sash, sleeves and cap. The Silk brothers, wealthy wholesale merchants of fruit and vegetables and owners of the champion Carbon Copy, had the colours Green, white band and armbands. Green and white had a certain amount of attraction for me, but these colours with a blue cap was something else again. That blue cap was no mere detail but spoke eloquently of its owner's taste for the unexpected and the unlikely. This might become clearer if I compare the Grimwade colours with a set that appeared often in New South Wales at the time. These were the colours of Sir Frank Packer, whose business was newspapers. Sir Frank's horses carried Green-and-white hoops with a red cap. The effect on me of those colours is wholly different from the effect of the green and the white and the blue. The red cap seems predictable, even crass, and the work of someone with a preference for making points by shouting rather than by persuasion. The blue cap, on the other hand—and it was a bright azure or sky shade of blue, rather than a dark shade that might have stood out more boldly against the green and white—seems to have been added not as a mere detail but as part of a pattern, and not to dazzle us but to invite us to look beneath the surface.

Surely I didn't derive all this from my first sight of Sanvo's colours? Probably not, but I was certainly much taken by them, especially when the owner of the colours and the horse had revealed himself as someone of immense patience and not a little cunning: someone who might have won several country races with his capable horse but who chose instead to have the horse run unplaced for month after month in the country so that he, the owner, might back it at outsider's odds in one daring attempt at a city race. On the day of Sanvo's dead heat at Moonee Valley, I began to assemble the first of the details that together comprise what might be called the legend of P. S. Grimwade.

All these things took place nearly sixty years ago, and I can't be sure today of their exact sequence. I'll finish this section by reporting, as they occur to me, my few memories of the career of my legendary figure.

I don't recall Sanvo's winning again during the year after his dead heat. What I next recall is my being at Caulfield on a certain Saturday in September 1958. In those days, two meetings were held at Caulfield in close succession: the first on the Saturday before the Royal Show Holiday and the second on the Thursday of the holiday itself. I was at Caulfield on the Saturday with Uncle Louis, and Sanvo was a fifty-to-one outsider in a field of good city-class horses. I explained to Louis my interest in the horse and its owner. Louis was one of the few persons who shared my interest in such matters, and we each had a small bet on Sanvo. The green and the blue and the white were obscured in the ruck throughout the race; Sanvo finished near the rear. Five days later, on the Show Day public holiday, I was alone at Caulfield. Louis had gone back to Warrnambool. Sanvo was engaged again. This time, the field was even stronger, and he was a rank outsider at a hundred-to-one. It was unusual for any horse to race twice in such a short time, and I should have been suspicious, but I had felt angry and humiliated in front of Louis five days before, after I had spruiked Sanvo to him and the horse had done nothing. I was in no mood to be enthused by Sanvo's chances. I had my standard bet on one of the favoured horses and ten shillings, win-only, on Sanvo on the tote. The field, as I reported, was stronger than the earlier field, but Sanvo seemed to be a completely different horse. He raced with the leaders throughout and fought out the finish with two others. The three passed the post with only a neck between them. The result, as it happened, was a dead heat, but this time Sanvo was not involved. Two very capable horses of those days were equal first: Droll Prince (Orange, white sleeves, red armbands and cap) and Brocken (White, ruby sleeves). A neck behind them, in third place, was Sanvo. According to the *Sporting Globe* of the following week, Sanvo's betting fluctuations on the Thursday had been fifties to a hundred and back to sixty-sixes. This told me that someone, or more than one, had gone along the rails late in the betting and had backed Sanvo to win a great deal of money for very little outlay. The bets had been lost, but not by much and, far from bemoaning the loss of my own piddling sum, I was ashamed not to have put much more on the horse so that I could have felt a solidarity with P. S. Grimwade in his misfortune.

One matter that told against P. S. Grimwade was the naming of his horses. Sanvo was by Sans Tache from Voucher. Paratone and Britain's Pride, to be mentioned shortly, were, respectively, by Paramount from Folkestone and by Great Britain from a mare whose name I've forgotten. I used to regret that the man I so admired seemed bound by the foolish custom of combining in his horses' names details from their parents' names. Perhaps I should have been more accepting and supposed that my admired owner was only acting in character. He had already given away through his expressive colours as much as he cared to give away of himself. Let him hide what was left behind the sort of racehorse names that many a lesser person might have devised. Paratone won a stayer's race at Caulfield one day at odds of twenty-to-one. Britain's Pride was a little before my time, so to speak. When I was in my last year at school, or it may have been a year earlier, the horse won a race at Flemington at fifty-to-one.

I can cite no other long-priced winners that carried the green and white and blue. I can report, however, that Sanvo got his name into the record books as the winner of the Moonee Valley Cup in 1959. He was the best of the Grimwade horses that I saw in action—too good, it seemed, to be restrained for month after month in preparation for a long-priced betting tilt. I seem to remember that Sanvo, during 1959, was placed in several races of good quality. He may even have won such a race in his lead-up to the Moonee Valley Cup. His ability was by now exposed, and he was never again at long odds. I was present when he won the Moonee Valley Cup, and I had only a small bet on him for sentimental reasons. He was one of the favourites.

I have no more facts to report about P. S. Grimwade or his horses. Given that the Grimwade colours were no longer seen on racecourses after the early 1960s, I wonder whether he may have been already an old man when I first became aware of his existence. If this is so, I very much regret that I'll never know how his horses performed when I was too young to be a follower of racing. Perhaps, on some afternoon in the years when I was only beginning to make sense of the sounds that so occupied my father when he sat by the wireless set of a Saturday, a horse owned by P. S. Grimwade achieved at Mentone or Williamstown what Sanvo came close to achieving at Caulfield on Show Day in 1959. I'll never know.

If I was at Moonee Valley when Sanvo won the Cup there in 1959, why did I not watch the trophy presentation and, perhaps, see in the flesh at last my legendary owner? I suspect I wanted to keep in mind the ideal man rather than have in sight the actual man. Or, perhaps I felt sure that P. S. Grimwade would have disdained to attend even such a meeting as included the Moonee Valley Cup and Cox Plate. Perhaps I wanted to think of him as someone for whom racing was better imagined than experienced—someone such as myself. Perhaps I assumed he was just then getting up from his cane chair on the return veranda of his sprawling homestead in the Central Highlands of Victoria. He had heard the radio broadcast of the Moonee Valley Cup, and now he had turned off the radio and was about to mount his hack and to ride out to inspect some of his cattle.

Why the Central Highlands? If I had not obtained evidence to the contrary, I would have envisaged P. S. Grimwade as owning an extensive property in what I consider the centre of the universe, in the quadrilateral bounded by Ballarat, Ararat, Hamilton, and Camperdown in the Western District of Victoria, which is a landscape of plains and low hills and vast skies. I've never felt comfortable when surrounded by steep hills, and I've tried always to keep away from mountains. But the scant evidence available tells me that P. S. Grimwade owned a cattle property somewhere between Broadford and Pyalong, about seventy or eighty kilometres north of Melbourne, in a district that I've never visited. I have a memory of having read once, in the *Weekly Times*, of a clearing sale or some sort of notable event on the property of Mr P. S. Grimwade at High Camp, which, according to my maps, is a district to the north of the Northern Highway not far short of Pyalong. I recall also that the last horse owned by Mr Grimwade before his name and his colours were lost to racing was called Glenaroua. The horse failed to win a race, but its name directs me to another district on my maps, a place about seven kilometres north-east of High Camp and far from any main roads.

I've travelled very little during my long life, but I've always enjoyed poring over maps. The district between High Camp and Glenaroua seems to be close to the watershed of the Central Highlands, which are a continuation of the Great Dividing Range as it peters out in Victoria. My maps show several creeks as having their origins between High Camp and Glenaroua, and a mountain of about five hundred metres in height is shown not far north-west of Glenaroua. I reckon I'm entitled to imagine my racing saint as having inherited old money but without any wish to display it; as having turned his back on Toorak and spent much of his life in a sort of lookout tower or eyrie, from which Melbourne and its surrounding plains are the merest blur of haze to the south; as having devised there his subtly eloquent racing colours; as having planned there his infrequent plunges on long-priced horses; and as having thus provided a man he had never heard of with abundant inspiration.

In the unlikely event that this book should be read by some or another descendant of a man named P. S. Grimwade, and that the descendant should wish to tell me that my account of the man is untrue, inaccurate, preposterous, whatever, I urge that descendant not to waste energy, time, or ink on the matter. Nothing will keep me from revering my saint as he was revealed to me.

16. *Who Saw Rio Robin?*

I GREW UP knowing hardly anything about alcohol. I connected it only with violence. In Bendigo, where I lived for four years of my childhood, our next-door neighbour used to come home drunk on beer of a Friday or a Saturday evening and used to beat up or threaten his wife and children. If I had to walk past one of the many hotels in Bendigo, I was frightened by what seemed to me an angry roar, although it was probably no more than the sound of twenty half-drunk blokes all talking at once. My father, his brothers, and their father were not fanatical teetotallers but drank hardly more than a bottle of beer or a glass of whisky at Christmas, although I've since heard that William Murnane, my great-grandfather, was a problem drinker, as we might call him nowadays. I have only the testimony of the puritanical Murnanes to rely on. Poor old William, or Bill, or whatever they called him, was a dairy farmer in a remote district, many miles from the nearest hotel. Why did he earn a reputation as a boozer? Did he drink a few glasses too many in a Warrnambool hotel during the weekly trip thither by horse and cart? Did he bring home a flask of grog and sip from it sometimes after tea?

I reckon I've drunk more in the last week than my poor ancestor drank in three or four months, but my aunts, his granddaughters, shook their heads at the mention of his name, whereas my grand-children have never seen me with a glass in my hand. (I have a glass of home-brewed beer beside me now, but my grandchildren are four hundred kilometres away!) If I had to point to a strand of boozers in my ancestry, I'd aim my finger at the Mansbridges. My father's mother was a Mansbridge and, although she would never have let a drop pass her lips, her brothers and her nephews were a thirsty lot.

During the many years when my father bet regularly with illegal SP bookmakers, he would have spent countless hours in hotels. Not all of this time would have been spent in bars. At the hotel in Sydney Road, Coburg, that was his favourite haunt, betting took place in a back laneway well away from the beer taps. But in Bendigo, during some of his boldest years as a punter, my father spent entire Saturday afternoons in hotel bars, surrounded by beer drinkers, while he drank only the occasional lemon squash. Only once did he come home affected by alcohol, although I didn't recognise his condition at the time. I was puzzled when he asked my brother and me three times in about fifteen minutes whether we had fed the chooks and collected the eggs. I was puzzled by his grinning at us while we ate our tea and his telling us several times what a fine family he had. I was even more puzzled by the strange sounds that I heard soon after I had gone to bed. My mother told me many years later that I had heard my father vomiting into the gully trap his evening meal and all the whisky that he had drunk during the afternoon while he was betting on the Melbourne races in one of the hotels of Bendigo. Why did he behave so much out of character on that one afternoon? And why did he make a mess of himself with whisky when he might have drunk beer or shandies? I still wonder sometimes about these matters.

Was it Mark Twain or Ambrose Bierce who defined alcohol as a substance that causes madness in the minds of total abstainers? Catholics were supposed to be tolerant towards alcohol, to say the least, but we had our few campaigners against Demon Drink. I know nothing of their origins, but there flourished during my secondary-school years a body known as the Pioneer Total Abstinence League, if I've recalled their title correctly. In the great days of the church, all manner of leagues and societies and confraternities and sodalities flourished, each with its special aim and each managed and promoted by one or another religious order. I gather that the total abstinence body had been entrusted to the Society of Jesus. Certainly, a Jesuit named Dando was the front man, so to speak. He visited schools and preached at confirmation ceremonies, always with the aim of having his hearers pledge themselves to a lifetime of abstinence from alcohol. I seem to recall that those who thus pledged were given a colourful certificate and a lapel badge. I moved so often from school to school as a boy that I was fifteen before confirmation caught up with me. I was confirmed by Archbishop Simonds, the coadjutor to Daniel Mannix, one Sunday afternoon in 1954 in Saint Joseph's Church, Malvern, which was full to the doors for the occasion. Father Dando, S. J., was given his timeslot and preached briefly but forcefully. Alcohol, he told us, was one of God's gifts and in itself neither good nor evil. Unfortunately, a great many people drank alcohol to excess, bringing harm to themselves and others and, of course, sinning mortally. Our lifetime of abstinence would make reparation to God for the sins of the abusers of alcohol. He urged all of us about to be confirmed to recite after him the words of the Pioneer League's pledge and, of course, to honour the pledge for the rest of our lives. I forget how we were to obtain afterwards our certificates and lapel badges, but no doubt he explained this at the time. Such was the volume of sound when the pledge was recited that every child in the church might have been swearing off the grog for life—every child except myself. As I wrote earlier, I knew hardly anything about alcohol. Drinking played no part in any of my frequent daydreams of the future. And yet, I did not take the pledge, perhaps because I've always avoided involvement in mass movements or demonstrations, or perhaps because I thought it unfair that I had to apologise to Almighty God for Great-grandfather William's occasional excesses. Surely most of those in the church that day became drinkers in later years, but they would have been less fortunate than I. Whenever, as a novice drinker, I woke next morning in misery, my remorse would have been only on account of the quantity I had drunk on the night before. They would have suffered in addition from the shame of having broken their childhood pledge.

I consider myself a controlled alcoholic. Some persons whose lives have been marred by alcohol might consider the phrase an oxymoron and might even be offended by my using it. I first heard it used to describe an expatriate Australian painter who lived out the last part of his long life in Italy. Every day during the last thirty or forty years of his life, the man sipped a measured amount of white wine from early afternoon until his bedtime. He lived well into his eighties. I've always disliked wine. I've drunk whisky or rum when beer was unavailable, but I've always diluted the spirits considerably. My preferred drink has always been beer and, for the past twenty years, my home-brewed varieties. I've seldom enjoyed drinking with large groups in hotels. In my first years as a drinker, the hotels closed at 6.00 p.m. Any beer bought before closing time could be drunk on the premises during the first fifteen—or, was it twenty?—minutes after closing time. Drinkers arranged themselves in so-called schools. Each member of a school bought in turn a round of drinks for the whole school. As closing time approached, those members whose turn to buy was approaching would buy their rounds in advance, so to speak. When the bar closed, each member of a school of four might have in front of him three glasses of beer, all requiring to be downed in the next fifteen minutes or so. In 1962, which is the year when this section of my book is set, I drank nearly every night in Frankston with a group of teachers and others and was often obliged to lie down for an hour after I had returned home from a session of what would now be called binge drinking.

After I was married, I seldom drank in hotels. Until my early middle age I had neither the time nor the money to drink more than a bottle or two of beer of a weekend, and this I drank always at home. After my sons had left home, in the early 1990s, I took early retirement and began to brew my own beer, which has an alcoholic content one and a half times that of standard beers. During the past twenty years, I've drunk a measured amount of home brew during almost every afternoon and evening—mostly alone, I'm not ashamed to report. I've had no illness to speak of since a bout of bronchitis more than forty years ago, and I've had to visit a dentist only once since I left school in 1956. I give myself a good chance of living for as long as that expatriate wine sipper, whatever his name was. As I said, I'm a controlled alcoholic.

I wasn't so controlled in 1962. In that year, I felt as though I had reached some sort of dead end or had painted myself into a corner. The year was my third as a primary teacher. When I had left teachers' college, at the end of 1959, my ambition had been to have several poems or short stories published in literary magazines within the next three years. In 1962, the third of the years was passing and I had had nothing published. Worse, I had written hardly anything. What was wrong with me, I wondered, and while I wondered I drank. And, for the first time in my short career as a racegoer, I began to drink at the races. This was something that my father and Teddy Ettershank considered a sort of degeneracy. But my father had died two years earlier, and who was Teddy Ettershank to me?

I was living and teaching in Frankston at the time. I had joined the Frankston Yacht Club as a social member. I've always hated and feared the sea, and I kept away from the yacht club on their sailing days, but on Friday evenings I got very drunk in their clubhouse and played carpet bowls until I couldn't see straight. On Saturday mornings, still hung over, I withdrew ten or twenty pounds from the State Savings Bank in Frankston (all banks opened on Saturday mornings in that long-lost golden era) and caught the train to

Melbourne and whichever racecourse was the site for the meeting of the day. By then I could afford to pay my way into the most expensive of the several enclosures, the paddock. I was respectably dressed in a suit and tie. (Jeans and tracksuits were never seen on racecourses then.) A Saturday program comprised always eight races. My practice was to station myself before the first race in one of the bars and to drink two glasses of beer while I studied the form guide and the race book. I did this before each of the seven later races. Admittedly, the glasses were smaller than the standard glasses served in hotels, but by the end of the day I had drunk more than enough to befuddle the skinny apprentice boozer that I was in my early twenties. What puzzles me most nowadays, when I get up several times in the night to empty my bladder, is how I managed to survive the long train trip home to Frankston every Saturday evening. I owned no car throughout the early 1960s, and no toilets were provided on the suburban trains. The journey from Melbourne to Frankston took an hour, and yet I always survived, with hardly any discomfort, until I reached the toilets at Frankston station.

I was very much a solitary at the races at that time. Dennis Hanrahan was already an assistant judge. Graham Nash was teaching somewhere, I knew not where, in rural Victoria. There would have been many Saturdays when I spoke to no one except the bank clerk who handed me my money in the morning and the bookmakers who took my bets in the afternoon. When I come to think of it, my whole weekend was spent in solitude, apart from my carousing with the yachtsmen on Friday night. On Sundays, I never left my comfortable flat but kept to my desk, sipping beer and trying to write something publishable.

Not surprisingly, I have few memories from the Saturday afternoons when I drank and bet and drank again. My one outstanding memory derives from a day at Flemington in late winter or early spring when I, who have always been ill at ease in front of an audience, took it on myself to pose to a dozen and more strangers, in the little old concrete stand that stood in those days just to the west of the members' stand, the question that gives this section its title.

For some weeks, I had been following a horse named Rio Robin (Dark-blue and light-blue diamonds, orange cap). Its part-time or small-time trainer was F. J. Stent from Flemington. I had backed Rio Robin twice already before the day in question. On each occasion, the horse had been most unlucky and had failed to get a clear run at the leaders in the straight. On the day when I backed him a third time, I had won much money on earlier races. I had backed Rio Robin at about ten-to-one in the last race, and I stood to win on him about forty pounds, or a fortnight's salary. Halfway up the Flemington straight, the horse was midfield but full of running, as they say. He was on the rails and needing to find a way through, just as on earlier occasions. Then the opening came; the horses in front of Rio Robin drifted away from the rails. My horse's rider did not hesitate but drove the horse through the gap. He seemed to me, for a few strides, the likely winner, but then the horses that had drifted outwards drifted back inwards. Rio Robin was severely checked and lost all momentum. The field pressed on to the finish, and my horse, for the third time in three starts, seemed to have been beaten by bad luck alone.

I've never looked for opportunities to make conversation with total strangers—not even when drunk. And yet, on that grey afternoon at Flemington, just after the horses had crossed the line in the last race of the day, I turned to my right and posed, in a loud voice and to a dozen and more men and women around me, all of them, I seem to recall, old enough to have been my parents, my urgent question. I wonder what sort of response I expected. Not only did no one answer me: they all looked studiously anywhere but in my direction and, if I hadn't been too drunk to have made such a subtle connection, their reaction might have reminded me of many an afternoon when some drunk would have been talking to the air around him outside a hotel in Bendigo and I would have crossed in haste to the other side of the street.

I was punished for my folly in a peculiarly appropriate manner. Rio Robin had his next start a fortnight later at Caulfield. When I first saw his name among the entries, I looked forward to backing the horse yet again at good odds and winning back my previous losses and more. When markets were published on the Friday, however, my horse was one of the favourites; and when I backed him on the Saturday, the best price I could get was eleven-to-two. Rio Robin won, but I had only a modest collect. It was as though every person who had heard my question at Flemington a fortnight before had noted the name of the horse I was ranting about; had read the stewards' report in the Wednesday *Sporting Globe*; had learned that the horse truly *had* been a certainty beaten; had told all their friends about the matter until, as the old saying had it, the dogs were barking Rio Robin's name all over Melbourne by the time when the horse next ran and the bookmakers, too, knew all about him.

17. *Palatial, the Dream-Horse*

LONG BEFORE MY wife's final illness, in 2008–09, one of her legs had begun to fail her. We had gone to the races on nearly every Saturday during the late 1980s and much of the 1990s, but towards the end of that decade we had to restrict our movements at racecourses. At Flemington, for example, she spent most of her time at one of the tables on the ground floor of the old Members' Stand. Recalling this, I'm able to say with certainty that I met Pauline D'Alton one Saturday afternoon in the late 1990s. She had taken a seat at the table where my wife and I sat, and had begun a conversation but had not introduced herself. After she had mentioned that she was the trainer of a certain horse that had run in an earlier race, I knew her identity. She was rather older than my wife and myself and, as she told us herself, ready to retire as a trainer. I was eager for her to know that I was by no means ignorant of her history. I told her that I had never actually seen her late husband but that I well recalled his sudden death many years before, when he had been in early middle age. I told her that my father had once told me that the smartest trainer in Melbourne was Alf Sands but that Artie D'Alton was not far behind him. (A. A. D'Alton was always known as Artie.) I let her know that her stable's colours (Yellow, blue sleeves) had been among the first that I had learned as a regular racegoer. We recalled together before we went our separate ways some of the better horses that she and, before her, her husband had trained but I made no mention of Palatial and neither did she. Had I forgotten that Artie D'Alton had been the trainer of my dream-horse? Or, had I thought it inappropriate to talk about prophetic dreams about horses with a hardheaded trainer, especially the widow of shrewd Artie D'Alton?

I'm not a mumbo-jumbo man. I've never been interested in meditation or karma or crystals or special diets, but I know what I know and, although I can't begin to explain what gives rise to dreams, I know that I've often dreamed about something that I've later experienced. I hasten to add that the events are almost always minor. I might dream, for example, that I've been confronted by a snake before seeing in the next day's newspaper a picture of someone with a pet python wrapped around him or her.

For someone who spends much of his waking hours thinking about horse racing, I've had surprisingly few dreams about it. I remember a great many of my dreams, but the only horse-racing dreams that I recall right now are three sets of recurring dreams, plus my dream of Gin Lane winning the Caulfield Cup and my dream of Palatial winning the Melbourne Cup.

The first of my recurring dreams used to come to me in the 1960s and the 1970s. I would be at a country meeting when several tall trees would fall to the ground on the far side of the course during the running of a race, usually when a field of horses was passing beneath them and with serious consequences. I ceased to have this dream after I had read a newspaper report (in the 1970s?) and had seen the accompanying photograph of a stewards' tower that had been brought down during a high wind at Hamilton while a race was in progress. No horses or riders were harmed, but the steward in the tower had had his leg broken.

Spain is a country that has never had any interest for me, but I used to dream that I had gone to a race meeting in Spain for the specific purpose of admiring Spanish racing colours, which I had heard were unlike any others. The only colours that I saw in the dream—or the only colours that I later recalled—were a set that looked from a distance as though they were All brown but turned out, when closely inspected, to be Chocolate-and-brown diagonal stripes. I've never had this dream since I learned, perhaps ten years ago, that a young horse in Sydney was carrying the extraordinary colours of Tangerine-and-orange stripes.

My third recurring dream still troubles me sometimes, and I can't imagine what actual event might bring it to an end. I'm at an important race meeting, and I'm anxious to watch a race that has just begun, according to the on-course sound system. My problem is that the so-called grandstand that I've entered in order to gain a view of the race is not your conventional grandstand with rows of terraced seats overlooking the course but a sort of vast castle filled with dining halls and staircases and gloomy corridors and throngs of people who seem unaware that a race meeting is in progress nearby. Sometimes, after struggling through a press of people, I get a glimpse of the racecourse through a narrow slit in the wall of a tower, but mostly I remain ignorant of what I would most like to know.

Gin Lane was a young horse of average ability when I dreamed, in the late 1960s, that he had won the Caulfield Cup. I doubt whether Gin Lane ever started in the Cup, but his full brother Beer Street won the race in 1970.

The setting of my dream about Palatial was one of those nightmarish and labyrinthine buildings where I struggled for a glimpse of race after race. At one point in the dream, I understood that the Melbourne Cup was in progress but I saw nothing of the race. I did hear someone far off in the crowd announcing that Palatial had won but I saw no official results—no judge's numbers displayed on high and no horses returning to scale.

The year was 1968. My wife and I were still childless and living in a flat in Park Street, Brunswick, overlooking Princes Park. I'd had very little time for reading form guides or race results during this or the previous two years. I was still a primary teacher but I was studying part-time for an arts degree, as was my wife. We seldom went to the races and, because we were saving for a deposit on a house, my bets were few and trifling. When I awoke after my dream about Palatial, I was aware that a horse of that name had raced in Melbourne in recent months but I could not have said whether or not the horse was a stayer or whether it was an entrant in the Melbourne Cup. I learned in time that Palatial was in the stable of A. A. D'Alton and carried the colours White-and-green diagonal stripes, gold sleeves and cap. The horse was a stayer of no more than moderate ability. It had been entered for the Caulfield and Melbourne cups but was among the least qualified of all the entrants and would be lucky to gain entry to either race.

I wish I could recall all the ups and downs of Palatial's career from June or July, when I first dreamed about him, until he ran in the Melbourne Cup in November 1968. Perhaps what interested me most was the question of why I had dreamed about Palatial in the first place. Every year, even when I was as busy as I was in 1968, I developed an interest in a number of entrants in the big cups and followed their progress during week after week. Palatial would never have been of interest to me if I had not, for some mysterious reason, dreamed of his winning the Melbourne Cup. As I said, he was not even qualified for the Cup when I first investigated him. And yet, he managed to become so. I don't recall his winning any race during his long preparation for the Cup, but he was placed in several. One such race was the Coongy Handicap at Caulfield, just before the Caulfield Cup. Palatial was required to win or be placed in order to qualify for the cups. He was what a racing journalist might have described as honest or a trier, and he struggled into third place in the Coongy and so remained in contention for the big races. I believe he started in the Caulfield Cup and ran his usual dogged race. He must have run rather well in one or another race leading up to the Melbourne Cup, given that he started at only twenty-five-to-one in the race that stops a nation. The field comprised twenty-six. Equal favourites were Lowland and Arctic Coast at six-to-one. The rank outsider was the Western District horse Dignify at 330-to-one. Palatial, at twenty-five-to-one, was equal fourteenth in the betting order and finished almost exactly where his odds had indicated—he was seventeenth of the twenty-six runners. The winner was Rain Lover at seven-to-one.

Why have I devoted a section of this book to a dream that fizzled out: a dud of a dream? The Melbourne Cup, as most readers will know, is run over 3200 metres, or two miles, as we used to call it. The race starts on the straight-six course, as we still call it, even in the decimal era. The field travels to the winning post and then around the whole perimeter of Flemington racecourse. So, twice during the running of the Melbourne Cup, one horse leads the field past the winning post. Rain Lover led the field by a spectacular eight lengths when they passed the post a second time in 1968. When they passed the first time, Palatial led them boldly. In his green and white and gold, my dream-horse was two or three lengths clear. It was no fault of Palatial, and certainly no fault of mine, that some ignoramus among the milling, jostling mob in the stairwells and corridors of my nightmare-grandstand—some ignoramus caught a glimpse, through a chink in a wall or over a parapet, of the Melbourne Cup field passing the winning post for the first time and then raised his false alarm.

18. *There Was an Emperor Napoleon*

FOR MANY YEARS now, I've listened to the radio only to hear an occasional description of a horse race, but things were otherwise in my childhood and youth. In Bendigo in the 1940s, my mother listened almost continually to our local station, 3BO. She was then a young woman in her twenties, and young women of her age nowadays would surely be amazed to learn that my mother's favourite singer was the tenor Richard Tauber and that her favourite songs included Tauber's versions of 'Pedro the Fisherman' and 'The Miller's Daughter'. In those days, no music seemed meant specifically for young persons. I may have been wrong, but I had the impression as a young boy in those years that popular music, what there was of it, was aimed at people in their thirties and forties. The first hit parade that I ever heard was broadcast from 3BO in 1948, not long before we left Bendigo, and I clearly recall my interest in the fact that the eight songs broadcast had an order of merit or popularity, as though they were contestants in a race soon to be run. I can still recall that the top of the hit parade, or the favourite in the impending race, was a song called 'Cruising Down the River' sung by a deep-voiced man named Arthur Godfrey.

Until the arrival of the hit parade, the music on 3BO had been of little interest to me: arias from operas; songs from operettas and musicals, as we'd call them today; and what used to be called *bel canto*. I was, however, interested in the hillbilly music, as it was called, that was broadcast, for some reason, in the early morning. I was like Clement Killeaton, the chief character of my first book of fiction, *Tamarisk Row*, in that I was moved to tears by the song 'There's a Bridle Hanging on the Wall', which was about a horse that died saving the life of its master.

After leaving Bendigo in late 1948, we lived for a year in a remote south-western district, with no electricity or radio. Back in Melbourne, in 1950, we found that hit-parade music, so to call it, in somewhat the way of rabbits and foxes and sparrows, had driven out the other varieties and was thriving all over the airwaves. This bothered me not at all. I listened to as many hit parades as I could. Much of the music was of limited appeal, but a few tunes, so to call them, had a lasting influence on me. When I wrote that last sentence, I had in mind 'The Roving Kind', sung by Guy Mitchell to the accompaniment of Mitch Miller and his orchestra; 'On Top of Old Smoky', sung, I think, by the Weavers with Gordon Williams and his orchestra; and 'Ghost Riders in the Sky', performed by persons long forgotten—by me, anyway. I'm still able to sing under my breath nowadays all of the melody and some of the words of each of the three songs just mentioned. I verified that statement by singing all three just now, and my next task is to try to explain why those and other popular songs so affected me all those years ago and why I've never forgotten them.

I don't think the words of the songs had much effect on me, although I may have taken note of the tone of a singer's voice or been moved by the crooning or the wailing of a choir. In fact, I had trouble understanding the words of many a song, and too many of those that I did make out were words to do with love, passion, desire, heartbreak—things that I believed I could readily imagine; things that I had already experienced in my limited, child's way; but things that I considered unsuitable for singing about and best brooded over or put into writing. I think that I probably got from my favourite popular songs what I would call rudimentary narratives, or perhaps even less than that—perhaps themes, or merely hints of themes of the sort that lie behind narratives. The things that I'm trying to describe are probably beyond description, but I've thought of a few titles that might hint at what I seemed to get from some songs. A certain song, for example, might have seemed to be telling me of *Clarity emerging from confusion*. Another song might have had for its deep message *Hope replacing despair*. Still another might have hinted to me of *Effort persisting in the face of failure*. Although I've found it hard to write about this matter, I was easily able, throughout my childhood and my teens, to think about it. As soon as I had heard a song for the first time, I knew whether or not it had a deep message for me and, each time I heard the song later, or each time I hummed it or heard it in mind, I understood a little more of the message.

When we tuned our wireless sets, we turned a knob and watched an upright needle move to the left or to the right behind a lighted panel of glass on which were painted the identification codes of the various stations. All Victorian stations had the numeral 3 followed by two letters, and most of the stations that my family listened to for news, music, and what we called serials seemed to be bunched near the centre or towards the right of the dial. Far to the left and rather isolated from all the rest were 3LO, 3AR, and a few regional stations that no one in our house ever listened to. These were the national stations, as we called them: the outlets of the ABC, or Australian Broadcasting Commission. If, out of curiosity, I tuned into one of the ABC stations, I heard either a male voice talking on some subject of no interest to me or a sort of music that had no message for me, being, so I thought, tuneless, repetitive, and interminable. (For a few years in my early teens, I was greatly interested in Sheffield Shield and, especially, Test cricket. I soon learned that the best descriptions came from the ABC, and I listened to them continually, but this in no way changed my attitude to their other programs.) On a couple of occasions, my brothers or I must have tuned into the ABC while my father was in the room and must have listened, or tried to listen, for a few minutes to some of the mysterious music that came from the far end of the dial. My father reacted with surprising indignation. He asked for the music to be turned off at once. He called it snobs' music. No one ever listened to such music for enjoyment, he said. The people who went to concerts and sat through hours of the stuff did so only so that they could boast afterwards to their snobbish friends of having heard Caruso or Toscanini. He pronounced the last syllable of the last-named so that it rhymed with *tinny*. Sometimes my father's opposition to a cause or a point of view made me inclined to defend it, or, at least, to investigate it. I felt no such inclination with ABC music, as I might have called it.

Hit parades proliferated through the early 1950s, although the sort of music heard on them would seem quaint today. One day in 1955, when I was in Form Five, a boy named Michael O'Dowd turned around from the desk in front of me and performed for me a rendition of a song that had won him completely: a song that would soon, so he said, be top of the hit parades. O'Dowd had heard the song in a film that he had seen recently: *Blackboard Jungle*. The title of the song was 'Rock Around the Clock'. The performers were Bill Haley and his Comets. The song would not only top the hit parades, as O'Dowd had predicted, but would change their content forever afterwards, but how could he or I have known this?

The new music did not take over all at once. In early 1956, I was much taken by a song that seemed to me one of the old sort: a song that I was able to relate to, as they say nowadays. I rejected the words and refused to sing them. ('There was an Emperor Napoleon / Who'd never heard of Nickelodeons...') Instead, I sang the stirring melody and waited for it to work on me. I was singing the melody in front of a boy named Brian Parker when he asked me whether I knew that my hit-parade song had been derived from a piece of classical music. No, I had not known what Brian was telling me, but my curiosity was aroused. Brian, it seemed, was well acquainted with classical music. (I learned the term from him and used it for many years afterwards.) Brian listened often to the ABC and persuaded me to do likewise.

For the next seven years, I spent roughly equal amounts of time listening to each sort of music. Instead of the half-hour programs presenting the top eight items of the hit parade, the commercial stations now had hour after hour given over to what became known as the Top Forty or the Top Fifty or even, I seem to recall, the Top Hundred. This sort of program occupied my attention in the late afternoon and early evening. Later, after the seven o'clock news, I would turn to the ABC stations and would listen until bedtime to their sort of music. In the early 1960s, I acquired a record player and began collecting a few records. I collected only classical music and never the other sort, and one afternoon in early 1963, for no specific reason that I can recall, I walked to the radio and switched off the Top Fifty program or whatever I was then listening to. Never during the fifty and more years since then have I paid any attention to popular music. Even in the 1980s, when my three sons often played their favourite music loudly in our house, did I make any effort to distinguish between U2 and Morrissey or their kind. Did I get those names right just then?

The reader may have supposed that this is another of those uplifting stories about someone who grew up ignorant of the world of serious music, who discovered its existence almost by chance, and who thereafter revelled in it for the rest of his life. No, this book, and every section in it, is about the world of horse racing, which has not yet been mentioned in connection with the Emperor Napoleon or with any other musical subject matter.

I first heard in Brian Parker's house in Glen Iris, in mid-1956, a recorded performance of the *1812 Overture*, by Peter Tchaikovsky, one or two themes of which had gone into the making of the popular song that had so impressed me—the song about the Emperor Napoleon. I was greatly impressed, but my hearing the overture in company—even in the company of a school friend—kept me from understanding why the music so impressed me. A year or two later, after I had acquired my own record player and my own recording of Tchaikovsky's piece and was able to listen alone to the music, I made a remarkable discovery.

I hope I can say that I'm not a boastful person, but if I were permitted to boast about one achievement or one characteristic of mine, I'd boast that I've never accepted any popular belief or theory without first testing it against my own experience or asking what possible relevance it could have for me. Expert commentators on serious music, as I'll call it from here on, would mostly have a poor opinion of the *1812 Overture*. The sort of persons who lose themselves in Beethoven's string quartets or Bach's fugues would probably smile indulgently or snort in derision if they were to read the following sentence. I esteem Tchaikovsky's *1812 Overture* far more than I esteem any of Beethoven's string quartets or Bach's fugues and I esteem the overture thus because, unlike any of the quartets or fugues, the overture, from its beginning to its end, brings to my mind a series of images comprising a complete narrative: a story beginning in early morning and culminating in late afternoon; the story of a notable and closely contested horse race.

I'm not going to try to explain in writing what I asserted in the previous sentence. I'm not going to try because I've come to accept that I've never met and will never meet anyone for whom horse racing matters so much. To put this another way: I've come to accept that of the millions of persons in this country who've listened at least once to Tchaikovsky's *1812 Overture*, I'm probably the only one who saw in mind while he or she listened a sort of mental film beginning before dawn on a remote country property where a man loads a racehorse into a horse float and ending, many hours later, with a scene in which two horses cross the finish line together. The scene is set in the 1960s, when the photo-finish system was in operation in Victoria but when the judge sometimes took several minutes to decide the issue in a finish that required him to await a developed print. (I've never understood the meaning of that technical term. I only know that the crowd used to be abuzz with speculation and the jockeys used to walk their mounts around and around in front of the grandstand while the judge awaited his print and afterwards looked at it through a magnifying glass.) Perhaps if I state only that the time between the horses crossing the line together and the judge finally signalling the result of the close finish is denoted, in my inter-pretation, by the passage towards the end of the overture in which a certain phrase is repeated several times, after which a certain note is repeated many times—perhaps if I state only this, then the astute reader may be able to acquire some notion of how the whole musical composition affects me, even today, nearly sixty years after I first began to understand the singular reason why certain pieces of music spoke to me and other pieces were devoid of relevance.

I probably wasted a hundred words and more on that last sentence. I'll spend no more words on trying to explain how certain passages of music evoke for me certain episodes in horse races. I'll simply end this section by listing some of the pieces of music that I most value for their evocative powers. No, I should explain first that I did not arrive easily at my understanding of the relevance for me of certain sorts of music.

After I had first seen in mind the complicated racing details provided by the *1812 Overture*, I supposed that this might have been a one-off: an isolated incident never to be repeated. For more than twenty years, I went on listening to serious music and to all sorts of so-called folk music, some of it probably authentic and much of it probably spurious. I knew all along that some of what I listened to spoke to me eloquently, whereas other music meant little or nothing. I was not unaware that my attachment to certain pieces had to do with their providing me with racing imagery. But the penny took a long while to drop. I forced myself to listen to Beethoven's string quartets and to some of Bach's most difficult music, still supposing that I was missing out on some precious secret available only to persons of superior sensibility. Nothing happened. The experience left me unchanged. I thought of my father's jeering at what he called snobs' music.

I can't remember when I accepted the truth: I had been listening to music all my life for the simple purpose of getting from it what I got from horse racing. I can't remember, but I suspect it was in the 1990s, when I had reached middle age and no longer felt that I had to learn from other people. I suspect it was in the 1990s that I twisted to my own purposes the statement of some old-time writer or pontificator, one of those so-called authorities that I was so much in awe of as a young man. I wrote in some or another published piece of mine that all art, including music, aspires to the condition of horse racing. I wasn't trying to be provocative. I was being honest.

Here, as a sort of appendix, are some of the musical compositions that I value most for the racing imagery that they bring to mind. The last few minutes of Beethoven's *Fantasia for Piano, Chorus and Orchestra* are an exact evocation of the last furlongs of a gruelling race. Each of the first and the final movements of Beethoven's Seventh Symphony brings to my mind a race contested by a horse whose fate concerns me. In the first movement, he is blocked as Rio Robin was once blocked. In the last movement, his apprentice jockey, following instructions, takes the horse to the front from the start and tries to lead throughout the race. Challenger after challenger appears in the straight, but the hero-horse holds them out. There's a symphony by Schubert—is it the Great or the Unfinished?—in which the first movement concludes with an exact evocation of what is often called a blanket finish. (The expression probably derives from someone's having said that the horses in the finish were so close that you could have thrown a blanket over all of them.) But my all-time-favourite piece of music, call it what you will—serious or classical or program-matic—is the first symphony by the Danish composer Niels Gade. When I first heard a recording of the work, I noticed at once that the last movement perfectly evoked the finish of a race full of meaning—well, the sort of meaning that people such as I get from racing. After I had listened a few more times to the symphony, I was able to derive from all four movements a complex series of images of landscapes and racecourses that the composer himself could never have anticipated.

A self-appointed critic of music wrote to me recently that Niels Gade is a romantic of little interest to him. The man who told me that will probably never read these words but I wish I could engage with him one day in a discussion as to what exactly takes place in the minds of people such as himself when they listen to what they call great music.

19. *Targie and Ladies' Pants*

IN DECEMBER 1953, I had almost reached the end of my fifteenth year. I had listened to radio descriptions of many hundreds of horse races, and I had read in newspapers the results of many thousands of such races. I had even seen occasionally in a cinema a brief black-and-white film sequence of the so-called highlights of some or another Melbourne Cup. And yet, I had still not set foot on a racecourse or watched any part of an actual race. I used to think this was the result of my parents' policy: they were trying to keep me from going the way of my father. I'm more inclined now to believe my deprivation was simply the result of circumstances. My father bet often but went to a meeting only if he had reliable information about one of the horses racing there. On such occasions, he would have preferred not to have his eldest son trailing after him. If I had looked more deeply into the matter at the time, I would have seen that my mother might have considered herself worse off than I. She had *never* been with her husband to a race meeting.

My first visit to the races was not even planned. At around midday on a certain Wednesday in the December mentioned, a car pulled up at our front gate in what is now South Oakleigh. In the back seat was Len Luxford, one of my father's best mates and a keen punter, although on a modest scale. Len, like my father, had no car, but he was being driven to the Mornington races by his son-in-law. The man's wife, Len's daughter, was in the front passenger seat, but Len offered my father a seat beside him in the rear. I'll never know who suggested there was room also for me.

Mornington in those days was surrounded by open paddocks and was considered a country town, but even country meetings attracted much larger crowds than nowadays, and we were late arriving in the car park. The first race was a hurdle race and I had been looking forward to watching it but, just as we walked through the entrance to the course, I saw, through the gap between the members' and the public grandstands, the bobbing caps of the riders as the field in the hurdle race came up the straight for the first time. That gave me the first of my several surprises at my first race meeting. The horses seemed to be travelling at breakneck speed. Whenever I had listened to a radio broadcast, I had supposed the horses to be ambling through the early stages of each race. Reporting this today reminds me of how removed I was from racing in the very years when I was becoming obsessed by it. Horses, jockeys, trainers, even the coloured jackets that so interested me—I had read about them or heard about them but never, or hardly ever, set eyes on them.

Had I not learned from those black-and-white newsreels mentioned earlier how fast a field of racehorses travelled? Seemingly not. Perhaps I assumed the image-horses in the newsreels had been speeded up like the image-persons in old silent films. Or, perhaps I forgot my brief sight of the Melbourne Cup field during the year that followed, when I would have spent hour after hour moving my glass-marble racehorses around the lounge-room mat so that a race could be prolonged for hours or even days.

I surely learned much on that first day at Mornington, although there were surely also a number of things that turned out to be just as I had expected them—the racing colours, for example, or the bookmakers' odds and the betting. I learned each of my two most memorable lessons from a particular horse. One was the actual mare Targie and the other was the imaginary mare Ladies' Pants.

Targie (Light blue, burgundy stripe and cap) ran in the last race of the day. I've forgotten her trainer, but her rider was Kevin Mitchell, who seldom attracted publicity but was an outstanding jockey for many years. Targie was second- or third-favourite in the race. The favourite was Great Caesar (Green, gold star—or was it a diamond?). Mitchell kept Targie just behind the leader until they entered the short, uphill Mornington straight. The rider of Great Caesar had kept his mount midfield and wide for most of the way. While Targie was about to pass the leader, Great Caesar was circling the field with a strong run.

As I prepare to write the forthcoming paragraphs, I'm reminded of the many debates, during the history of Christianity, on the subject of free will and predestination. I was once able to make myself slightly dizzy by trying to reconcile the opposing views, as I understood them. Sometimes, it seemed to me that if God was all-knowing and if He foresaw all of human history, then human beings were incapable of making free choices; all they could do was to follow whatever course of action was already mapped out for them. But sometimes, I could convince myself that human beings were indeed free. At any moment, a person was able to decide between several possible courses of action and so to alter his or her future. In this scheme of things, however, God seemed reduced in stature. How could He be all-knowing and all-powerful, if human beings—His mere creatures—were making up history as they went?

The above may seem far removed from horse racing, and yet I've observed myself over the years changing from someone whose view of racing was that of a predestinarian to someone who stands on the side of free will. Probably because I saw no actual races until I was nearly fifteen, I tended as a boy to think of each race as predestined. When I looked through a field of horses of a Saturday morning, I felt as though I was merely trying to see in mind the results of the race as they were going to be printed in the Saturday evening edition of the *Sporting Globe*. I might seem to myself sometimes to be weighing up the claims of various horses, but God or Destiny had done this already, and the race would be run so that the preordained winner actually won. This was the sort of thinking, by the way, that drove many punters to search for the perfect betting system. The researcher of systems, having found, let us say, that horses carrying top weight and starting favourite won twenty-five per cent of the races they contested in a given year, would assume that such horses would register exactly the same achievement in any later year.

I hadn't been a regular racegoer for long before I came to understand that no race result should be thought of as inevitable; that the best a punter can do is to pick a horse that seems to have a winning chance and to hope that the horse has good luck in running. Even if the Almighty, in the vast Grandstand in the Sky, knows all the winners in advance, He knows too that in many a race an eventual second-placegetter was being hailed as the winner twenty metres short of the post.

I don't remember whether I had tried to select the winner of the last race at Mornington on that day in 1953. I would have been still a predestinarian, and if I had selected Targie I would have supposed, a few seconds after the field had straightened, that I had correctly worked out what God had known through all eternity. Kevin Mitchell had driven the mare to the front. None of those immediately behind her was making any ground. She seemed safe. Kevin Mitchell, though, seemed not to share my theological views, or perhaps he knew what a strong finisher was Great Caesar. Mitchell took to Targie with the whip—not flogging her but keeping her mind on the job, as one racecourse expression would have put the matter, or making a good thing of her, to use another such expression. And well he might have whipped the mare, for Great Caesar—whose rider had sat quietly rounding the turn, perhaps to let the horse keep its balance—was now finishing fast.

This was only my first day at the races, but I could see that Great Caesar would beat Targie, even when he was still a length or two behind the mare. The favourite drew level twenty or thirty metres out and quickly passed Targie. And then, still three or four strides short of the winning post, Kevin Mitchell put away his whip. I must have been watching him intently, for I can call his actions to mind with absolute clarity and have done so many times during the last sixty years. Mitchell looked across at the colours on the jockey just then passing him. Then, with a surprisingly graceful gesture, he changed his grip on the handle of his whip so that it rested near the mare's shoulder while he rode her with hands and heels towards the post. Whether he was a believer in predestination or whether he argued for the operation of free will, his graceful gesture seemed his way of saying that he had done all in his power and could do no more.

A few hours before I had learned from Targie to question some of my beliefs about racing, I had been offered a lesson in quite a different field of knowledge. I used the word *offered* advisedly. The lesson took place, but I doubt whether I learned much from it. Or, rather, I doubt whether I've profited much during my lifetime from whatever I learned that day at the Mornington races.

A good-sized crowd was on course. On the grassy slope overlooking the winning post, people stood shoulder to shoulder before each race. I watched most races alone. My father and Len Luxford liked to stay in the betting ring until the last few minutes, whereas I liked to have a good view of the races. Before one of the main races, the persons nearest to me on my right side were two or three young women. I have no recollection whatever of the appearance of the young women or of what they would have been talking about in my hearing. I was a gangling boy of nearly fifteen. Even if the persons beside me had seemed only three or four years older than I, I would have thought of them as mature women and of myself as a mere boy. Even if they had seemed to be of my own age, I might not have met their eyes. I had not even spoken to any female of my own age for two years.

In 1951, I'd had a girlfriend for most of the year. We were only twelve years old, she flat-chested and I still in short pants, but we were comfortable together. By early 1952, my family had moved to the opposite side of Melbourne and I was attending an all-boys school. We lived in a suburb of mostly new houses occupied by couples with infant children. I don't recall even passing any girl of my own age in the streets of my suburb.

Not long before the start of the main race, a young man positioned himself just in front of me. He may have been one of a group of two or three—I don't remember. He seemed to be of about the same age as the young women and, although they were obviously strangers to him, he set about getting their attention. His chief target was the young woman nearest him, who was also the one nearest me. I was embarrassed and kept my eyes on the horses milling behind the barrier, which was not far away at the top of the straight.

Races in those days took a long time to start. This was before starting stalls came into use. The horses were supposed to walk in a line towards a barrier consisting of rubber strands that could be released into the air at short notice by the starter. Sometimes, a field of horses would be behind the barrier for five minutes before their riders could get them to walk forward together. During this time, if the race was being broadcast, the commentator would have to fill in with naming the troublemakers or making small talk until his sudden cry of 'They're racing!' or 'They're away!' or 'They're off!'

The young man in front of me began imitating a racing commentator while a field was behind the barrier. If I had known what he was up to, I would have pushed my way into the crowd and fled the scene. But I had no suspicion of what he was about to say and, anyway, his patter was brief and he reached his punch line with hardly any preamble. 'Peter Pan, Carbon Copy…' He named a few of his imaginary horses…And I'm sure today that he would have locked eyes with the young woman on my right while he said, 'Ladies' Pants…they're off!'

During the remaining minutes before the field was off at Mornington and during the two minutes while the race was run, I dared not look at any of the young persons around me, and as soon as the field had passed the post I made off into the crowd. I had looked at none of the young persons, and I was so uncomfortable that I never afterwards recalled any sort of conversation that may have begun among them. I neither looked nor heard, and yet I somehow sensed the atmosphere and was amazed to find that it seemed not to have changed. Not only had the young woman not slapped the face of the young man nor sent one of her companions in search of a policeman, but there seemed to be between her and the young man the same easygoing mock-wariness as before. How many days or weeks passed before I understood that I was the only person in our little group who had been shocked by what was said?

20. *Elkayel and the Enzedders*

I'VE MENTIONED THE New Zealanders already. They baffled me. I used to try to outwit them but I mostly failed. Sometimes, as I tried to explain earlier, I was driven to suppose that the cunning of the New Zealanders consisted in their following a wholly predictable course of action while conspiracy theorists such as myself awaited the unfolding of convoluted plots. At other times, their deceptiveness, or what I might have called their old-fashioned crookedness, fooled me completely. I can hardly believe it today, but after having decided, in early October 1960, that Eric Ropiha's Ilumquh (Black, green Maltese cross and cap) had been set to win both the Caulfield Cup and the Melbourne Cup, I dropped off the horse, as the saying goes, after it was beaten at short odds in a lead-up race to the Caulfield Cup. What was I thinking? Ilumquh won the Caulfield

Cup at double-figure odds and would have won the Melbourne Cup but for interference.

I was alerted to Even Stevens (Gold, emerald-green band, red cap) in 1962, but I stupidly put a lot of money on him at his first Australian start. The race was at Caulfield in the week before the Cup. I've never seen a rider use less vigour than the rider of Even Stevens used that day. If the jockey had sneezed in the straight, the flashy chestnut would have won, but he didn't—I mean, neither did. I backed Even Stevens in both cups and collected, but he was at very short odds. His connections had put their money on weeks before, when no one knew anything about the moderately performed horse. I won barely enough to cover my losses from that first dead run.

I'm calling them the Enzedders in this section. My friend David Walton, who might fairly be called a social animal, would always use that term when introducing my wife and me to some or other New Zealanders that he had invited to the numerous gatherings that he organised. 'This is So-and-so and his wife, So-and-so,' David would say. 'They're Enzedders.' I was always disappointed to find that the Enzedders at David's parties knew nothing about racing. Or, did they only say that to keep me from suspecting that they were in Australia as undercover agents for some fiendishly secretive stable at Wingatui or Awapuni?

The year 1964 was a significant year for me. I had left Frankston and was living and teaching in the inner suburbs of Melbourne. In the first weeks of the year, she who had been my girlfriend for the past few months had cast me off, so to speak. This turn of events hardly surprised me. Nor was I surprised when my first day at the races as a bachelor brought me outstanding profits. The day was Oakleigh

Plate Day, one of my favourite days at Caulfield. The Oakleigh Plate is run mostly on a hard track, but in 1964 rain fell all day and the track was sloppy. I've forgotten how I did it, but I backed five of the eight winners, including Pardon Me, the winner of the Oakleigh Plate. The horse's trainer was a man named Bede Horan from Sydney, and its colours were a combination of gold and black and red. The Oakleigh Plate is a keenly contested race, but I felt almost from the start that Pardon Me would win. He seemed to be cruising or coasting in fourth or fifth place down the side of the Caulfield track. I remember Oakleigh Plate Day in 1964 as one of the few days when I felt as though I had learned at last how to make money from racing.

The year 1964 promised to be a year of regular race-going and perhaps the sort of profits that I had been trying for years to achieve. The spanner in the works was my having met up with, at my new school in the inner suburbs, a certain young woman who had been at teachers' college with me five years before. I'd had no interest in her at teachers' college, but five years had wrought all sorts of changes in the universe, and I asked her out, to use that quaint old expression, in midyear. I took her to the races at Caulfield, and we got on well together. Four months later, when the Spring Carnival was underway, we had made no formal announcement, but we seemed to have agreed that we would eventually become engaged and afterwards marry.

As if all that was not enough, I had made a solemn promise to the young woman, my future wife, that I would enrol as a part-time, mature-age student in an arts course at the University of Melbourne. My course would occupy all my spare time for several years to come. I would have no time for writing poems or short stories or the beginnings of novels. I would probably not even have time for reading form guides or betting on horses. My betting might be curtailed also by my need to save towards the deposit for a house. My girlfriend and I had only modest bank accounts, and eligibility for the federal government's grant to buyers of first homes depended on regular saving.

Without any prompting from Catherine, my girlfriend and future wife, I resolved to give up betting. I mentioned no period of time. I knew in my bones that my vow could never be permanent. One day I would come back to the punt, but for now I would deposit in our home-savings account each week the sum that I would previously have bet on the Saturday races. My vow would come into operation immediately but with one modification or exemption. The time of year when I made the vow was late October. The Caulfield Cup had only just been run, and the Melbourne Cup was a couple of weeks away. Under the terms of my vow, I was allowed to have one last bet on the Melbourne Cup.

I seem to remember that the entries for the big cups in 1964 included fewer than the usual numbers from New Zealand. Even so, I considered only New Zealand horses when making my final selection for the Melbourne Cup. I looked forward to having my last bet for the time being, if not for all time, on an Enzedder and, of course, on collecting. Not only would I win good money—I'd have the satisfaction of having worked out the Enzedders' plans.

Selecting my horse seemed easy enough. With hindsight, I understood that I should have been suspicious, but one horse seemed to stand above the others. This was the six-years-old gelding Elkayel. He had been placed in the Caulfield Cup, as had many Melbourne

Cup winners during my lifetime. The other New Zealand horses had moderate form and, even allowing for the Enzedders' noted cunning in these matters, I could not foresee any of the other horses improving sufficiently to beat Elkayel, whose trainer I've forgotten, but whose jockey was Grenville Hughes wearing a combination of green, blue, and yellow.

It seemed appropriate that my farewell bet should be a good-sized one. I took twenty pounds to Flemington on Cup Day to put on my selection. I got half my bet on at tens and half at twelves, so that I was set to win 220 pounds. I happen to recall that a new Volkswagen Beetle cost about a thousand pounds at the time; my winnings would have been a useful addition to our home-savings account. Those odds, by the way, made me a bit uneasy. They seemed to me twice what should have been on offer. If I had been setting the market, I would have had Elkayel favourite at six-to-one. Betting markets, however, just like other markets, are affected by supply and demand, and Elkayel was not greatly in demand. Had I been better informed, I might have noted the significant demand at long odds for another six-years-old New Zealand gelding. This was Polo Prince (Gold, emerald-green hooped sleeves and cap), which had run fairly in his lead-up races and close up in the Mackinnon Stakes without attracting my interest. I seem to have supposed that Polo Prince had been fully extended in all of those races, which is a supposition that should never have been hastily made about any horse from New Zealand in the years that I'm writing about. Maurice Cavanough, in his book *The Melbourne Cup 1861–1982*, reports that Polo Prince firmed from twenty-to-one to twelve-to-one with leading bookmakers on the day before the Cup. Cavanough adds that the owner of Polo Prince later denied having put any money on his horse—but an Enzedder would say that, wouldn't he?

Grenville Hughes was described as a leading New Zealand jockey, but I would have described his ride on Elkayel as incompetent. (That would have been my description during the days after the race. Later, when I had begun to entertain certain dark suspicions, I might have said that Hughes had ridden a perfectly judged race.) Hughes allowed Elkayel to drop to the rear of the field of twenty-six. At the far side of the course, halfway through the race, Elkayel was a hundred metres and more from the lead. Admittedly, the leader was a tearaway outsider, but I never expected my horse to win. Elkayel was still nearly last at the top of the straight. He then began to pass horse after horse with a strong run wide out, but I could still see that his task was impossible. While all this had been happening, Polo Prince had stayed near the lead. At the top of the straight, while Grenville Hughes was angling his horse, without any seeming haste, towards the outside of the field, Polo Prince dashed clear. He was still in front at the post, but Elkayel had got to his rump after having given him an impossible start.

That might have been the end of the story, and those might have been the only facts available for my pondering in all the years since, but a few months after the Cup I met at a social gathering a man who worked for a rails bookmaker. The man told me—not as though he was revealing some dark secret but as though he was repeating what was already common knowledge in the circles he mixed in—that yes, a great deal of money had been won at long odds on Polo Prince, and that the people who had won the most were what he called the Elkayel connections.

21. *Summer Fair and Mrs Smith*

FOR MANY YEARS, I read *Time*, the weekly newsmagazine, from cover to cover every week. I stopped when Time-Life, or whatever they called themselves, came up with an Australian edition. I could learn all I needed to know about Australia from newspapers or from magazines such as the *Bulletin*. What I had especially enjoyed in *Time* was the coverage of people and events far from Australia, but this was much reduced in the Australian magazine, and they lost my custom for good. But in earlier years, I read everything in *Time*: everything from reports of military coups in Togo or Equatorial Guinea to descriptions of new art galleries in Tucson or Baltimore or new trends among football cheerleaders in Austin or Green Bay. I mostly read the magazine when I was on trams or trains during the years when I preferred not to own a car. I was reading it one evening on a crowded suburban train in the early 1960s, when a sentence at the end of an article in the Books section brought on a fit of giggling. I was a man in my early twenties, but I had to cough and frown and bite my lip and to think of serious things so as not to make a fool of myself in the crowded compartment.

I had been reading a review of a book called *The Bachelors*. This work would have been the book-length equivalent of those articles that appear often in women's or men's magazines describing some or another emerging trend or some increasingly popular lifestyle. The author had filled chapter after chapter under such headings as 'Bachelors and Interior Design', 'Bachelors and Sex', 'Bachelors Who Live Together'—that sort of thing. The reviewer had found the book interesting enough and had enlivened the review with some witty observations of his own. He had tried to end on a light note, and it was his last sentence that had set me off in the train. The sentence was roughly: *One quirky custom unites all the many and varied sorts of men described in this book; all bachelors, it seems, urinate in sinks and washbasins.*

I lived at the time in a tiny place that had been advertised as a flat but was really a single room with a gas ring and a stainless-steel sink concealed behind a door in the corner. I lived there during all of 1961 and part of 1962, and through all that time I urinated in the bowl of my kitchen sink, but there were mitigating circumstances.

My room was a converted back veranda behind a double-fronted solid-brick house that still stands today and is still numbered 50 in Wheatland Road, Malvern, near Tooronga Road. One wall was part of a rear wall of the house with the bricks painted over. The gas ring and sink were at one end of the room, at about the midpoint of the rear of the house. A small window was above the sink, but I kept the curtains drawn across it because it came close to making a right angle with a much larger window in the rear wall of the house. This large window, I guessed, was the kitchen window for the occupants of the house.

The occupants of the house were not the owners. The whole place belonged to Mr and Mrs Jakubowicz, a middle-aged couple who lived somewhere in Windsor and who called at Wheatland Road every Sunday morning to collect the rent from their tenants. They had told me from the first that the rent must be paid in cash, and I always obliged them, but Mrs Smith, co-tenant of the house with her husband, John, told me once of her attempt to offer Mrs Jakubowicz a cheque. According to Mrs Smith's account, the land-lady had gone all funny.

The landlords had three rents to collect every Sunday. In the backyard, not far from my covered-in veranda, was a tiny bunga-low that served as a bedsitting room for the Ortlieb couple, a young husband and wife who had come to Australia as children of German migrants and talked often of going back to their homeland. They worked as cutters or machinists in a lingerie factory. The Ortlieb couple, unlike myself, had no gas ring or sink in their bungalow. Their kitchen occupied a third of another building, little better than a shed, at the rear of the backyard. The kitchen made up the central third of the shed, as I prefer to call it; one of the outer thirds was a bathroom and laundry that I shared with the Ortliebs. They and I shared also the other of the outer thirds of the shed. This third was a toilet, clean and serviceable but separated by only a weatherboard wall from the Ortliebs' kitchen. Sometimes, of a

Sunday morning, when I was taking my week's washing towards the laundry, I would see the Ortliebs still at the breakfast table in their tiny kitchen but would not hesitate to fill the washing machine and set it going. Sometimes I showered while the Ortliebs were on the other side of the wall. Never, during the year and more while I lived in Wheatland Road, did I go into the toilet while the Ortliebs were in their kitchen on the other side of the weatherboards. I somehow managed to regulate my bowels so that they never needed to be relieved during the Ortliebs' mealtimes. As for my bladder, I relieved it as often as needed—in my sink beneath my little curtained window, making sure always to run the tap at the same time and for some time afterwards.

I kept away from the Ortliebs and their endless grizzling about the poor pay and conditions in their workplace. I would have kept away from Mrs Smith too, but she seemed to know in advance when I would be at the letterbox or walking down the side path and would come out of her front door and keep me talking. She and her husband, John, were a childless couple in their forties or fifties. I saw him sometimes leaving early for work. He was certainly not a white-collar worker but I never learned what humble job he did. She stayed at home all day and had hardly any visitors. I wondered why they rented a house much larger than they needed. I gathered from things she let slip that she had inherited a large house and, perhaps, even a farm in the Shepparton district and intended one day to return there. When I think of her now, I think of the phrase *old-fashioned*. Perhaps because she had never brought up children, her ways and manners seemed to belong to an earlier decade. I'm pretty sure she addressed me by my first name, but she was always *Mrs Smith* to me.

Mrs Smith alone was not at all hard to put up with, but I began to think of moving elsewhere whenever Glenys was around the place. I don't know whether I've spelled her name correctly but Glenys was a girl perhaps a few years older than myself who sometimes stayed with Mrs Smith of a weekend. Glenys, if you're reading these pages more than fifty years after we last met, you'll probably be offended by my describing you as a plain-looking young woman, but you'd surely concede that you were never going to offer yourself as a Miss Australia candidate. Yes, I've written my harsh words now, and I'll have to let them stand. Glenys was a plain-looking young woman. She was also like me in being something of a loner. When a person from Glenys's and my age group spent Saturday evening alone, it raised the strong possibility that he or she was without a boyfriend or girlfriend. Glenys seemed to turn up every few weeks at Wheatland Road and to spend the Friday and the Saturday evening alone with the Smiths. Mrs Smith would surely have observed that I myself was alone on those evenings. I was without a girlfriend during the whole of my time at Wheatland Road, although I had occasional visitors—mostly solitary males like myself but sometimes an engaged couple that I knew and once, for a few hours, a young woman that I had hoped might become my girlfriend. I should add that although I spent most of my weekends alone, I never considered myself an object of pity whereas I tended to feel sorry for Glenys. I went to the races every Saturday. I had no fridge where I could keep beer cool, but I bought supplies of rum and mixed it in equal parts with Schweppes lime cordial to make a palatable and heart-warming drink. I spent my evenings sipping my mixture and reading. Sometimes I even wrote a little. I would never have said that I was living my ideal life, but after I had drunk a certain amount of my rum-and-lime I supposed I was very soon to meet up with a compatible young female person. I even supposed she might have been sitting just then as I was—alone and in need of company. But I never supposed that she was Glenys, who might have been sitting just then on the other side of our dividing wall.

I spoke to Glenys once—more than once. Mrs Smith caught me with my guard down on one of the first occasions when Glenys was visiting Wheatland Road. Before I could think of an excuse, Mrs Smith had got me to have afternoon tea on her front veranda with Glenys and herself and—strangely, it seems to me now—a young woman from next door. The surname of the young woman was Monk, and whereas Glenys and I were introduced to one another by our given names, the neighbour and I were introduced to one another by our surnames, and even Mrs Smith addressed her as *Miss Monk*. As I said earlier, Mrs Smith was oddly old-fashioned.

I have no recollection of what was talked about at the tea table but nor do I recall any uncomfortable silences or embarrassing gaffes. Still, if Mrs Smith had hoped that I might afterwards have asked Glenys to take a turn with me around the front lawn and might have asked Glenys while we walked if she cared to go to the races with me next Saturday, nothing of the sort happened. Though Glenys returned every few weeks to Wheatland Road, she and I remained as far apart as ever.

This book is supposed to be about horse racing, and yet the races have hardly been mentioned in all the preceding pages of this section. I'll shortly introduce Summer Fair, winner of the famous leg-pull AJC Derby at Randwick in October 1961. Before then, I have one last thing to tell about Glenys. One fine and warm Sunday morning after Glenys and I had each slept alone in our solitary beds on the Saturday night under the same roof but separated by several walls, I heard from just outside the window over my sink the sound of the back door opening—Mrs Smith's back door. Next, I heard the clattering of high heels on the concrete path leading to the clothesline that all three tenants shared. The line was bare at the time. I must have brought my own washing in earlier. Perhaps I was leaving my washing until later in the day. Anyway, the high heels belonged to Glenys. She clattered to the line and then used a pair of pegs to suspend from the nearest wire a pair of ladies' pants, briefs, whatever you want to call them. That was all. She hung the things there in the backyard, on the otherwise empty clothesline, and then clattered back to the house. She had on her face the sort of fatuous half-smile I had sometimes seen there. It was one more of the things that prevented me from becoming interested in her.

So, now I had something novel to look at: a centre of attention in what had been an empty backyard. Now, there dangled in the breeze this cute little item of ladies' underwear. As I recall, the colour of the item was steel grey or, perhaps, pale blue. There was not much substance to the item. I mean, they were a brief pair of pants, to put it plainly. They were not exactly opaque, either. In another context, they might have been described as *revealing*. Anyway, there they hung, somewhat to the mystification of the solitary young man who was staring at them from his bachelor's lair. I've mentioned already in this book that I've always had the greatest difficulty understanding the behaviour of females, especially when it has to do with romantic or sexual matters. I could not even be sure whether Glenys's hanging out a pair of pants on a Sunday morning was any sort of message. But supposing it *was* a message, what sort of message had she hoped to get from me in return? Not that I had the least intention of replying to her lingerie-bunting. I had been trying for months past to make it clear to Mrs Smith and to Glenys that I was not interested in the young woman. But this seemed an opportunity to improve my skills in dealing with young females. I felt obliged to consider what I *might* have done if I *had* been interested in Glenys and wanted to respond to her message.

What was I expected to do? Should I walk out to the clothesline and stare up at the things as though imagining them clinging to the hips and groin of their owner? Should I feel them? Should I *steal* them—lift them down from the line and carry them off to my room, there to wait for her to claim them and not to return them until she had paid the price of a kiss? Perhaps I should rinse out a clean pair of my own Jockey underpants and hang them on the nearest line and parallel to her undies, so that the breeze lifted each item towards the other in a series of airborne pelvic thrusts? It was all so crazy. I drew the curtains across my windows and went on with my reading or writing.

And now for Summer Fair! I'm somewhat ashamed to report that I can't recall his colours. I recall only a predominance of red with markings of white or pale blue. I don't even know whether he was a gelding or a colt but, like every other person who followed racing in 1961, I recall that Summer Fair won the AJC Derby of that year on protest. He had been beaten across the line by Blue Era (Red, black-and-white striped sleeves, black cap) but his rider, Tom Hill, had protested that the rider of Blue Era, Mel Schumacher, had held him, Hill, by the leg as the horses approached the line. This was verified by the stewards after they had seen film of the race. Summer Fair was promoted to first, and Mel Schumacher received a long suspension for foul riding.

At that time, I had a friend in a senior position in the Victorian Railways. He told me, soon after the AJC Derby, that the Railways had been asked to provide customised transport between Sydney and Melbourne for the young racehorse Summer Fair which, for some reason, could not endure road travel. My friend told me in addition that someone connected with Summer Fair had whispered to someone in his, my friend's, office that Summer Fair was coming to Melbourne to contest the Caulfield Guineas, which he would not win, and afterwards the Caulfield Cup, which he would most assuredly win. I thanked my friend for his information and resolved to have a small bet on the three-years-old in the Cup. My friend was not a racing man, and I had never put much faith in second- or third-hand tips.

Summer Fair ran well in the Guineas without winning. That need not have meant that his connections had had the horse deliberately beaten. The Guineas was a race over 1600 metres. The AJC Derby, run not long before, was over 2400 metres. The large difference in distances could easily have caused Summer Fair to be beaten on his merits in the much shorter Guineas.

On Caulfield Cup Day, 1961, I was in a reserved box in the grandstand. I had been invited there by a former colleague at the Royal Mint, where I had worked four years before. Warwick Murray had known nothing about racing but had become a part-time punter after noting the achievements of Martin Dillon, whom I've mentioned several times already. Reserved boxes were a recent innovation at several Melbourne courses. They seem primitive now, when diners sit at terraced tables behind glass, but I felt I was sampling the latest in luxurious living while I lolled against the canvas walls of our little enclosure and sent the waiter scurrying for cold beer after cold beer. Before the Cup, I went down into the ring and had a pound or two on my fancy, whose name I've forgotten, although I remember that its rider was George Moore; its colours were predominantly purple, with orange-and-white markings; and its odds were about six-to-one. I recall also that it finished near the rear in the Cup. The horses were on their way to the barrier before I remembered Summer Fair. I had come to the races intending to have five or ten shillings on the three-years-old but had forgotten all about the bet. I went in search of the nearest tote window. When I found it, the young woman across the counter told me that the minimum bet was a pound. This was in the part of the grandstand occupied exclusively by reserved boxes. We loungers in the boxes were deemed by the club, it seemed, to be above betting in shillings. I must have had a fair amount of beer by then. I was not going to be thought a cheapskate by the young tote employee. I bet a pound win-only on Summer Fair. The young horse had been about twenty-to-one with the bookmakers, but, for whatever reason, he lacked for support on the tote. He won the Cup with not much trouble and paid forty-to-one on the tote. I had won the equivalent of three weeks of my teacher's salary on him.

Summer Fair was not my only winner that day, and I left the course more than fifty pounds better off than I had entered it. My lean-to in Wheatland Road was less than two kilometres from the grandstands at Caulfield. My custom was always to walk to and from Caulfield on race days. I walked without interruption *to* the racecourse but on the way home I stopped for two or three or four or five beers in Macnamara's Caulfield Club Hotel. If I had won a goodly amount, I sometimes bought the smallest crayfish on sale in the fish shop near Macnamara's and devoured it soon after arriving home. The crayfish had to be small, and I had to devour it soon because I had no fridge in my quarters.

I don't recall having bought a crayfish after Summer Fair's Caulfield Cup, but I do recall having drunk more than my usual amount of beer at Mac's, as it was familiarly known. I don't recall walking home. I don't even recall the first and by far the most urgent task that I would have had to perform after having entered my little apartment—my hurrying to the sink and emptying my swollen bladder. Afterwards, I would have run a copious amount of water down the sink, but I recall none of this. What I do recall is my sitting down in the middle of the room and counting out my winnings. Even though I could hardly claim to have backed Summer Fair as a result of my own assessment of the field, what mattered was the end result, and I took pleasure in counting out the wad of notes in my pocket.

Nothing else from that day stays in mind. What I next recall is my meeting with Mrs Smith a few days later. Was it an accidental meeting, or had she ambushed me at the letterbox or in the driveway? Mrs Smith was not a racegoer, but the Great Age of Racing was still not quite at an end and suburban wives such as Mrs Smith still kept abreast of racing results in the spring and autumn carnivals. I don't recall which of us mentioned the Caulfield Cup, but I can never forget my telling Mrs Smith that I had won a goodly sum on Cup Day and her replying that she knew this already; that she and Glenys had overheard me from the kitchen of her house on the evening of Caulfield Cup Day while I counted out my winnings.

Excuse me, as they say nowadays, or used to say recently. Here we have Mrs Smith and Glenys poised with ears pricked in their kitchen while the young fumbling drunk in his room nearby flicks the corners of his banknotes. Now, what is the comparative loudness of a man's flicking the corners of a few banknotes in the middle of his room with the same man's pissing furiously from a bursting bladder into a stainless-steel sink in the corner of his room nearest to a pair of huddled, listening females? Even while Mrs Smith was talking to me about my success with Summer Fair, I understood that I had been sprung. My shabby secrets were known. It was time to think of moving on.

22. *Sir Flash and the Borderers*

THE FAMOUS THREE-DAY racing carnival at Warrnambool in May attracts visitors from all over Australasia. In the 1950s, and for a few years afterwards, a lesser two-day carnival was held in January, complete with hurdle races and a steeplechase. It could not be compared with the May event, but good crowds attended, many of them holidaymakers staying in Warrnambool or other coastal centres. I was like most people in associating Warrnambool with the ocean, but I had never taken much interest in the flat sandy beaches around the city. My father's family had been settled for nearly a century in the Mepunga district, about twenty kilometres east of Warrnambool. There, the coast consists of tall cliffs broken occasionally by small coves and bays. As a boy, I enjoyed climbing among the fallen boulders and the rock pools at the edges of some of these bays, but the ocean itself repelled me, and I've kept well away from it during all of my adult life. During my brief holidays on my grandfather's farm in the 1940s, I was more interested in another sort of ocean. Whenever I stood on a tall cliff above some or another bay, I got inspiration not from the blue-green Southern Ocean reaching away towards the South Pole but from the yellow-brown ocean of land reaching towards places I had seen only from a distance, if at all: the plains of the Western District to the north and the north-east of Warrnambool or, away to the north-west, a mostly level landscape where I had never been and where the towns were for me mere names on a map—Hamilton, Coleraine, Casterton...

I have always delighted in the atmosphere of the mounting yard. Nowadays, a concern for safety has resulted in owners and trainers and jockeys having to confer before a race in a railed enclosure well away from the parading horses, but for many years I could look into the mounting yard before a race and could see, in the open space bounded by the circling horses, knot after knot of persons, each surrounding a brightly clad jockey. Before a race, anything could be deemed possible. The shortest-priced favourite might be beaten; the rank outsider of the field might get up in a photo finish. The claims of no contender could be dismissed. The plans and tactics being discussed among any one of the knots of people might soon come to fruition, and the colours displayed at its centre might finish ahead of all the others. Those colours, I need hardly say, had a special interest for me when I saw them in the mounting yard before a race. I could read all sorts of things into sets of racing colours before a race. One set might seem to boast; another to issue a challenge; and still another to make a quiet but firm statement. I was easily able to see some sets of colours as representing particular regions or places or even something as vague as a way of life. And, of course, any set of colours was first of all connected with a trainer or an owner: a weather-beaten veteran trainer or a fresh-faced newcomer; an owner new to racing or someone from the third generation of an old racing family—someone using colours devised by his grandfather.

I was leaning on the mounting-yard fence one day at Warr-nambool during the summer meeting when I saw a man whose image comes easily to my mind today, sixty years later. I long ago forgot the man's name; nor do I recall anything of his trainer or his jockey. His horse was named Concito, and I remember the colours it carried, although I found them unattractive. I've sometimes tried to persuade myself that every possible set of colours must, by definition, be distinctive and must have a certain amount of appeal, but I've never been able to bring myself to like a certain few combinations of colours. One of them is the combination of black, red, and light blue. Concito's colours were Black, light-blue hoops and sleeves, red cap. At least, the preponderance of the light blue made the colours a bit more appealing than a combination of mostly black and red. The owner of Concito was the best-dressed man in the mounting yard. This was a country meeting, where some owners and trainers wore neat casual dress, as we call it nowadays, but the owner of Concito wore a suit of some expensive-looking pale material, a white shirt, a tie of mostly pale blue with touches of black and red, and a grey hat with feathers in the brim. Even more striking than his clothes was his silver hair—or what could be seen of it beneath the brim of his hat. And there was plenty to see. Most men still favoured short back and sides in the 1950s but this man, like some of the wealthy residents of Toorak who I saw at Metropolitan Golf Club when I worked there as a caddy, obviously wore his hair long, so that it was bunched above his ears and neck.

Nowadays, a trainer's hometown or suburb is printed after his or her name in the race book, but that was not the practice in the 1950s. My only way of learning where Concito was trained, and so to learn the district where its owner might have lived, was to look at its form in the race book: to see where it had raced recently. The horse's three most recent starts had been at Hamilton and Casterton in Victoria and at Bordertown in South Australia. Even after having learned these facts, I was still a long way from knowing where exactly Concito came from. A triangle with those three named towns as its apexes covered a large slice of countryside, but my lack of specific evidence was hardly a hindrance to me. At the next opportunity, I unfolded a map of the far west of Victoria and the far south-east of South Australia and set not only my eyes but my imagination also roaming. At that time I had been no further north-west of Warrnambool than the township of Koroit, only a short drive inland, but I was able to recall a few illustrations from the *Weekly Times* and the *Leader*. I might also have performed a sort of extrapolation, telling myself that the country further inland must have been by degrees drier than the coastal zone. I guessed that the landscapes I was assembling in my mind were no less level than those I had seen from the coastal cliffs, although any place on a map that had winding roads or the beginnings of watercourses reminded me to include a few hilly districts or plateaus in my private territory.

I called the territory the Border District and its inhabitants Borderers. I awarded to those inhabitants not only the usual

amount of shrewdness and sagacity attributed to people living far
from the capital cities but extra doses of cunning and acquisitive-
ness on account of their living close to a border. When I did this, I
had in mind vague memories from my reading in history books of
parties of Welshmen driving home English cattle from across the
border; of wily Pyrenean peasants profiting from smuggling; of the
Percy men lording it over Northumberland and southern Scotland.
My Borderers did not literally smuggle or steal livestock. No, they
used horse racing to achieve what the Welsh and the Pyreneans
achieved by less subtle means. Their living near the edge of things
made them more circumspect and painstaking than racing men
from the coast or from around Melbourne or Adelaide. The long-
range plans of Borderer owners and trainers more often succeeded.
They more often landed their betting plunges. I would not have
my Borderers thought of as wholly devoted to gain, however. They
numbered among them many a man who wore his hair bunched
above his ears and on his neck and who stood out on a racetrack
on account of his elegant dress and proud bearing. Such a man
owned a vast cattle or sheep property and lived in a mansion with
a veranda on three sides and groves of deciduous trees all around.
His mansion included a library and a study. The walls of the study
were covered with photographs of the finishes of races won by his
own horses. The walls of the library were covered, of course, with
books, and while I could never dare to suppose that even one of
the many mansion owners in my vast border district sat sometimes
at a table in his library trying to compose a local variant of one
of the renowned Border Ballads, still I like to think that many a
mansion owner read sometimes from a collection of those ballads

and considered them, as I do, as eloquent and memorable as any poems in our language.

No plunge was launched on Concito. The horse finished fourth or fifth, but this may have been part of some long-range plan that culminated, months later, in a successful plunge at Edenhope or Penola. I never heard of the horse again. Nor did I ever hear again of another Borderer, Sir Flash, or of his connections, who bore far more resemblance to Welsh cattle thieves or Andorran smugglers than did the silver-haired owner of Concito.

The story of Sir Flash (Green, pink cap) is simply told. The horse may even have competed at the same meeting as Concito. Certainly, the meeting was in January at Warrnambool. I was with my father, who was constantly stopping to talk to some or another old acquaintance from the district or even to a few visiting smart men from Melbourne. The talk always concluded with each man's giving the other one or more tips for the day and, although no one from Melbourne mentioned him, most of the locals wanted to tip Sir Flash to my father. Several of them added, however, that they doubted whether the horse would actually run that day. They raised this doubt because the horse had still not arrived at the course even a couple of hours before the starting time of its race. My father and I verified this by visiting the stall allotted to Sir Flash in the so-called birdcage and finding it still empty.

Sir Flash must have arrived on course just in time, given that he took his place in the jumpers' flat in mid-afternoon. Few jumpers' flat races are run nowadays. They were interesting races, usually over a long distance and reserved for horses that had completed the course in a stated number of hurdle races or steeplechases within a stated time before the race. Sometimes, an astute trainer—to use an epithet much liked by racing journalists—would start a moderate flat-racer in a series of jumps races, not caring where the horse finished but only that it should complete the course and thereby become qualified for a jumpers' flat race. Most jumping horses were plodders on the flat, and the astute trainer's horse might have had an advantage after he had been transformed legally from a flat-racer into a jumper.

My father's acquaintances were not the only ones who expected Sir Flash to run well. The bookmakers, too, had had their ears to the ground. A large field contested the race, but Sir Flash opened at the short odds of five to two. That was the best bet against him. There was no sudden, well-organised plunge—just a steady flow of money. My father and all his tipsters had good bets on Sir Flash. Even my father's Melbourne friends joined in with their bets. Although there was no plunge, my father pointed out to me two men who went continually to bookmaker after bookmaker, sometimes two or three times to the same one. The men had moderate bets of twenty or forty pounds each, but their total outlay would have been considerable. My father had never set eyes on the men, and no one that he knew from around Warrnambool knew anything about them, but you know who they were, and so do I. Yes, they were Borderers.

I had not then learned to observe the behaviour of horses and jockeys during a race, but my father told me after Sir Flash had won by two or three lengths that the jockey had spent most of his time in the straight trying to stop the horse from winning by three or four times its eventual margin. It may have been my father or Uncle Louis or someone else of their acquaintance who first muttered that

Sir Flash may well have been a ring-in. Correct weight was duly declared, but the considerable number of people who went to the birdcage to see the horse rubbed down were surprised to find that Sir Flash had been led straight from the course. This in itself was suspicious, and the more so when people recalled that the horse had not arrived at the course until shortly before its race.

Stewards' practices sixty years ago were lax indeed by comparison with today. Every horse had its distinctive brand, and its registration papers described its natural colour and markings. Plus, a steward was supposed to go around the birdcage long before each race, asking to inspect the registration papers for each runner and comparing what was on the papers with what was on the horse. And yet, who knows what short-cuts a steward may have taken at a meeting at Warrnambool on a hot day in the early 1950s? Who knows how carelessly a steward may have looked at a forged set of papers or an altered brand? Perhaps a lazy or hasty steward may have waved his hand indulgently after some agitated trainer or strapper had told him that the papers had been left by mistake in a car at the far end of the car park, or that the horse had still not arrived on course because its float had broken down on the other side of Warrnambool? If the city performer Regal Vista was successfully rung in for the poorly performed Royal School at Casterton in 1972, why could not Sir Flash, twenty years before, have been not the horse of that name but the winner of open handicaps at Murray Bridge or Gawler or even Morphettville?

Ring-in or not, Sir Flash took much money from the bookmakers that day, and the horse's connections got their share of it. They would have taken their winnings in a north-westerly direction.

After the race, one of my father's acquaintances, annoyed that he'd had only a small bet on the horse, jabbed his finger at the printed summary of Sir Flash's form in the race book. What sort of jumping races had the horse contested, the man wanted to know. By what right had this dashing flat-racer got himself entered in a race for jumpers? He read out the information that Sir Flash had started most recently in a jumping race at Apsley, in far-western Victoria, and before that in a similar race at Penola in South Australia. My father's friend was not alleging that Sir Flash was not the horse that had finished unplaced in two weak jumping races. What he seemed to be saying was that jumps at Apsley and Penola were lower or easier than at other courses and that the connections of Sir Flash had somehow cheated their way into the race at Warrnambool. He seemed to be blaming a bunch of Borderers for doing what any horse's connections would have done if they had had half the chance.

After my wife had died, a few years ago, I moved to a small town in what some would call the north-west of Victoria but I like to call the far west. The town lies outside the pointy triangle made by joining up the places where Concito had three consecutive starts many years ago—but not far outside. This is definitely Border Country. And yet, the Borderers are not like the folk I imagined in the years when some of their number brought horses to the summer meeting at Warrnambool. Since I moved here, I've been to race meetings at Mount Gambier, Penola, Naracoorte, and Bordertown in South Australia, and at Edenhope, Casterton, Horsham, Nhill, and Murtoa in Victoria. I've seen much good racing. I've heard, while leaning on the fence of many a mounting yard, absorbing exchanges between owners and trainers and jockeys. What I've seen and heard, however, seems to suggest that most connections can only hope for success. No trainers or owners in this far-reaching district seem even to plan, let alone bring to fruition, the sort of coup that my Borderers of long ago brought, or were supposed often to bring. Even the betting is on a much-reduced scale. I've watched owners or trainers walk from the mounting yard after their horse has gone onto the track and bet twenty or, perhaps, fifty dollars on it with one of the few bookmakers fielding. For heaven's sake! Fifty dollars today wouldn't equal a pound in 1960, when I began as a primary teacher. I used to take five or ten pounds to a race meeting. My bet would be ten shillings or a pound. That's either twenty-five or fifty dollars at least in today's money. But I was so ashamed of my small bet that I would never have approached a leading bookmaker with my miserable stake. And now I see owners or trainers betting what I was ashamed to bet as a young teacher who lived from pay cheque to pay cheque.

I've learned much about racing from the meetings I've attended here in Border Country. I've seen tough-looking men and women brushing away tears after their horses have won maiden races with a first prize of only five thousand dollars. I've seen part-time trainers or owner-trainers lovingly grooming and then leading back towards the car park some horse that has started thirty times for one win and a few placings. I've seen much more that I feel privileged to have seen, but I've seen hardly anything of what I would have expected to see if someone could have told me in the 1950s that I would one day live among the Borderers and would observe them from close at hand.

So, this section of my book is just another variation on the old theme of the grass's being greener on the far side of the hill—or, is it? In 2012, the publisher Michael Heyward, whom I've known for thirty years, expressed an interest in visiting me here, near the border. He wanted not just to see how I was surviving here but to observe the district and some of the people who live here. Michael arrived here in the hot days of late January with his wife, Penny Hueston, and William and Anna, two of their adult children. I was pleased to show them Lake Ratzcastle, to take them to the top of Mount Arapiles, and to serve them each a drink in the tiny clubhouse of our local golf club, where I'm bar manager. Then I had a brainwave. Driving around the district, my guests and I had seemed mostly to be looking from the outside inwards. It was time to look at the district from the inside, so to speak.

I phoned my friends Andy and Clare Robertson. Yes, they would be happy to show me and my Melbourne visitors around Pleasant Banks. The visitors and I drove a few kilometres along the road that leads to South Australia. I had driven often past the huge property of Pleasant Banks but had never seen the homestead, which is far back from the road. I had never seen the sprawling stone building, with its long verandas overhung by wisteria and grapevines, but it was exactly as I had seen it in mind when I had looked north-west from the coast sixty years before, imagining the way of life of the border dwellers.

After morning tea, Andy and Clare offered to show us around the many-roomed house. The visitors from Melbourne followed Clare around, but I got no further than the first room along the hallway. It was called the billiard room, but I took no notice of the green-topped table or the rack of cues. I went from wall to wall, peering at the dozens of framed photographs. Six generations of the Robertson family have farmed in this district, first on the old Mortat pastoral run and later at Pleasant Banks. They were not only farmers but breeders and owners of racehorses. On the walls of the billiard room were pictures taken at racecourses all over south-western Victoria and south-eastern South Australia and showing winner after winner owned by Andy's father, Peter, and other family members. The family colours went back for several generations—Gold, purple sleeves and cap. In later years, the Robertsons' trainer had been K. G. Davis from Naracoorte in South Australia. And yes, in answer to my hesitant question, Andy had assured me that his father had liked a bet, preferably at each-way odds.

I had long ago admired the connections of Sir Flash for their daring raid on Warrnambool. The Robertsons of Pleasant Bank had raided as far away as Melbourne. I saw a black-and-white photograph of a hurdle racer owned by Andy's grandfather. The photographer had caught the horse in midair, soaring over an old-style batten hurdle. It was the last hurdle of the race, and the Robertson horse had a winning lead at Flemington ten years before my birth and in the great days of the Borderers.

23. *Sacred Heart Cathedral, Bendigo*

SURELY A DOZEN years at least have passed since I last saw Bendigo. Maybe I'll never see it again. If I do, though, I'll be sure to spend some of my time there as I've spent some of my time whenever I've visited the city since I left it nearly seventy years ago—I'll call at the Sacred Heart Cathedral in Golden Square; I'll enter the building from near the main entrance in Wattle Street; and I'll sit for a few minutes in one of the back pews, not meditating and certainly not praying but just watching whatever images occur to me. And, if no images occur to me at once, or if an overly long interval occurs between the appearance of one or another image and its successor, then I'll simply look around me at the amazing light inside my favourite building.

I've sometimes wondered whether my childhood experiences

in Bendigo are largely responsible for my never having wanted to travel. How else to explain why I've never been on aeroplane—why I've never been further from Melbourne than Murwillumbah, in New South Wales, to the north; Kettering, in Tasmania, to the south; and Streaky Bay, in South Australia, to the west? My wife and I had serious differences in many matters, but she and I were united in our dislike of travel or tourism. Sometimes, after our three sons had left home, and when the month was January and half the people of Melbourne seemed to have found somewhere better to be, Catherine would ask me whether we should go away for a few days. Even if we failed to enjoy our few days away, she would explain, we could at least tell our friends and neighbours that we had *been* away, instead of having to explain, as we usually had to, why we never took holidays. My answer was always the same: the only place that I had any desire to visit, apart from the racecourse that was the venue for the next Saturday meeting in Melbourne—the only place that tempted me to leave my desk was Bendigo.

Occasionally, we did take a daytrip to Bendigo. Catherine had a friend there, a woman who had been widowed in early middle age. Catherine's friend sometimes offered to show us around the city, but I would always put her off. All I wanted to do in Bendigo was to sit for twenty minutes in Sacred Heart Cathedral. Once, I consented to stroll with Catherine and her friend under the elms in Rosalind Park, the same trees that I had walked beneath on memorable days of my childhood. Yes, the trees were the same, but the motor traffic in Pall Mall and View Street and Williamson Street kept me from feeling any connection with the mostly quiet city where I had lived from 1944 until 1948.

Even the ordinary sunlight on a fine day in Bendigo could set me daydreaming, but the light inside Sacred Heart Cathedral was something else again. It was a refinement or a distillation of the light outside. On the day when I first arrived in Bendigo in January 1944, I made a fanciful connection between the strange new light all around me and the gold that had been responsible for the founding of the city and its continuing prosperity. I supposed that the special quality in the light above Bendigo was somehow the result of the sunlight's having been reflected from the countless specks of yellow in the quartz pebbles strewn on the footpaths of all the back streets of the city.

In earlier years, I could not have found words to account for the influence on me of the light in the cathedral; I was only able to feel a sort of pleasant suspense, as though about to experience something that was more than daydream but not so unalterable as actuality. In more recent years, my way of responding to the light has been to hear in mind, or to see in mind, as though on the page where I was startled to read them for the first time when I was nearly forty, the words attributed to Paul Éluard: *There is another world, but it is in this one*. And then, because no abstraction, no matter how seemingly profound, can satisfy me for long, my mind is occupied by imagery. I sometimes wonder what sort of imagery was in Paul Éluard's mind whenever he pondered on his profound statement. It was probably very different from the stuff that fills my mind on such occasion. I've never read that Paul Éluard was the least bit interested in horse racing.

One Sunday morning in September 1948, I was kneeling at intervals and at other times standing or sitting while solemn high mass was being celebrated in Sacred Heart Cathedral, Bendigo. My father was beside me. My mother and my two younger brothers were at home. Perhaps they were attending one of the masses at St Kilian's, which was our usual church. I don't remember. Two things should have puzzled me that morning, but I seem not to have given them much thought. First, I should have wondered why my father and I had walked two kilometres from our house in Neale Street to the cathedral when St Kilian's was only half that distance away. The other matter was that my father had often declared that he disliked the tedious ceremony of a high mass. My father was a faithful Catholic but hardly a devout one. The nearest he ever came to advancing a theological argument was his occasionally arguing that God was surely more pleased to be honoured by the simpler ceremony of the so-called low mass than by the music and incense and the bowings and scrapings of a high mass. He also lacked the docility and the obsequiousness that so many Catholics of that era accorded the clergy. He approved of priests who visited the sick and the poor but had little admiration for those who hobnobbed with the doctors and lawyers of their parishes.

And yet, there we were, he and I, on that fine spring morning, sitting through a high mass that was interrupted often by the organ and the choir and by the to-ings and fro-ings of the several sumptuously robed co-celebrants, one of whom might have been the bishop himself—probably not frail old McCarthy but his truculent coadjutor Stewart. (I should never speak harshly of Stewart. He was derided in later years as an archconservative but it was he who oversaw the work that made the cathedral complete. When I lived in Bendigo, and for many years afterwards, the building still awaited its spire.)

I was sometimes devout as a child but more often lax, although never tempted to rebel or to disbelieve. During my devout periods, I would try to pray during mass; during my lax periods, I would daydream. I was daydreaming for much of the morning while my father and I were in the cathedral.

My daydream took the form of a narrative. I had read few books at the time. The sort of narrative most familiar to me was the radio drama. On many a night, after having asked my mother's or my father's permission, I was allowed to listen to a fifteen-minute or thirty-minute program on 3BO in which the voice of a narrator and two or three other voices enacted a dramatisation of what had probably started as a chapter in a book of popular history or an item in an encyclopaedia. I can recall hearing a dramatised account of the mystery of the *Mary Celeste* and another of the discovery of anaesthetics. Medical history seems to have been a fertile source of such dramas. I recalled just now my hearing an account of William Harvey's cutting up of the family parrot in his search for proof that blood circulated rather than lay around as one of the four humours. Anyway, while the bishop sat in his canopied chair beside the altar, or while the other two priests were wielding the thurible or the aspergillum, I was composing a radio drama having as its subject my father, Reginald Thomas Murnane, of whom I was rather fond and whose many flaws and faults had not yet become apparent to me.

Music was an important part of every radio drama, and I may even have been moved to set about composing my own drama after having heard some especially plangent passage from the huge cathedral organ. My theme was my father's progress from an insignificant babe-in-arms to a person of considerable importance, which was what I took him for at the time. I knew hardly anything of my father's life story. I knew he had been born at Allansford, which is now almost a suburb of Warrnambool but was then a mere township on the Hopkins River and the last station on the railway line from Melbourne to Warrnambool. I knew he was the third of nine children and the oldest boy among them. His younger brothers had never left the district around Warrnambool, but my father had left home and had travelled all over Australia before marrying in his mid-thirties. When I, his oldest child, was born, he had been a warder at Pentridge Prison. He had moved to Bendigo to be the Education Department's attendance officer for the city and for much of northern Victoria. It was a modestly paid post, but it required him to visit many large schools, to inspect the attendance rolls, to confer with head teachers, and to interview the parents of truants. Many of these he had to summons to court, and on the day of their court appearance he had to act as prosecutor. He was a talkative, affable man who made friends easily. Another sort of man might have crept into and out of the head teacher's office in the many schools that he visited but my father enjoyed taking morning tea with the whole staff in most of the many schools in his jurisdiction. There was also his career, so to call it, as a racegoer and punter. I knew hardly anything about his losses, but I recalled the many evenings when he had come home with crayfish and ice-cream and the family had feasted after one of his big wins. While I passed the time in the cathedral, I merely noted rather than organised the wealth of subject matter available for my radio drama and tried to imagine the powerful impression it would make on its many listeners. As I've said, I was daydreaming.

My dramatised story would have followed an upward trajectory, so to speak. I did not learn for many years afterwards that the man beside me in the cathedral that morning was at one of the lowest points in his life. My parents had been hinting for some time that we might soon leave Bendigo for the Western District. My brothers and I were warned to say nothing of this at school. We were actually excited by the prospect of a move to the region where we spent our holidays. Although, for much of my later life, I've thought of Bendigo as a lost golden paradise, I was not at all dismayed, in 1948, at the prospect of leaving it forever. And after we left, only a few weeks after the morning of the solemn high mass in the cathedral, our moving into a dilapidated house from which my brothers and I had to walk more than three kilometres to school seemed more an adventure than any sort of family tragedy.

I learned the simple truth many years later from my mother. I should have worked it out long before, but where human behaviour is concerned I'm the least perceptive of persons. I should have understood long before that my father's moving from Bendigo to the Western District at the age of forty-five could never have seemed anything but an admission of utter failure, either to himself or to his siblings and his parents and to those who had known him as a young man. He had left his father's dairy farm more than twenty-five years ago. He was not going to follow the gruelling life of a dairy farmer, even if it should lead, as it led for his brothers, to his one day acquiring his own farm. Who knows what exactly he looked forward to when he left home—travel? adventure? a wife and children? new friends? wealth? He certainly gained the first four but not, alas, the fifth. Whatever pretences he might have adopted, it would have been absolutely clear to his family and to anyone in the district who gave any thought to the matter that my father's arrival in Mepunga East from Bendigo was no triumphal homecoming but its stark opposite. The house we moved into was on the way to becoming derelict, the sort of house that passing children throw stones at or nickname the Ghost House. My father could not afford a car. While even the poorest farmer in the district chugged around in some sort of 1930s jalopy, my father's sole means of travel was an old pushbike that he had found in the junk room of his parents' farmhouse. He rode the bike five kilometres every morning before daylight to the farm of a widow whom, as it happened, he had known since childhood and who would have been well able to appreciate his comedown. He milked her cows morning and evening and did labouring jobs between times. He was a share farmer, on the lowest rung of the social ladder as it was envisaged by all in the district.

And why had he come to this? Because he had bet beyond his means—not once or twice but again and again while he chased his losses, and not in cash, which might have been bad enough, but on credit and with a pair of bookmakers who could almost have been called friends of his: the Bourke brothers, my father's fellow parishioners at St Kilian's, on the corner of Chapel Street and McCrae Street in Bendigo.

Dear old St Kilian's! If, during a word-association exercise, someone should fire at me the word *church*, I would fire back the words *St Kilian's*. But that's part of another story. In *Tamarisk Row*, the boy Clement sometimes begged his father for the price of a malted milk so that he, the boy, could enjoy his frothy drink in the shop across the road from the church and could escape the boredom of having to stand in the shade of the date palms in the churchyard while his father and a half-dozen racing men talked endlessly about races already run and races still to be run. Among the half dozen were fictional versions of the Bourke brothers. I have a vague recollection of two ginger-haired, easygoing men. How was I to know, on the morning when my father led me by a roundabout route well clear of St Kilian's to the cathedral in Golden Square, that his sole reason for doing so was that he could no longer face the Bourke brothers? How could I have known, while I idled away my time in the cathedral, that the hero of my radio drama had led me to that place of golden light and soulful music only in order to hide from his bookmakers, the men that he was soon to welsh on?

24. *Mary Christian Murday of the Same Address*

I'VE MENTIONED ALREADY in this book that I've hardly ever enjoyed watching a film. The notion that people reveal their true selves by talking, shouting, rolling their eyes, or otherwise gesturing seems absurd to me, who have tried all my life to use speech and body language in order to conceal rather than reveal. I have long believed that a person best explains himself or herself when writing to a reader, either real or imaginary. Nevertheless, and although I've probably watched fewer films and stage plays than anyone of my age and cultural background, I can still recall a few images that I've watched and I'll admit that those images have been of value to me.

It may have been as long ago as the 1970s when my wife, who did not share my poor opinion of film and the theatre, persuaded me to watch a film version of what had been originally a stage play. The title was *Separate Tables*, and the playwright was, I think, Terence Rattigan. I recall that the plot was intricate—far too intricate for me. The characters were mostly residents of some sort of boarding house or guesthouse. Some, I seem to recall, were singles while others were couples. While the action went forward, all manner of tensions arose among the various characters. Only one resident of the place seemed unaffected by these tensions. This character was a mannish-looking woman who sat alone every morning while the others arranged themselves in different groups according to the subtle dynamics of the play. Whenever the camera picked her up, she was sitting alone and taking no notice of her fellow guests or even of the food that she was eating, and all the while she was putting pencil marks on a newspaper, which the viewer had previously learned was the paper that published form guides every day for every race meeting in Great Britain.

I know nothing of the craft of writing scripts for film or live theatre, but I soon understood that the woman hunched over her form guide was a foil to the main characters. While they were falling in or out of love or forming or breaking down alliances, she was utterly removed from their concerns. She was a marginal character, but she came into her own in a brief scene towards the end. By then, the tensions between the leading characters would have been palpable for a discerning viewer such as my wife. I would have lost the plot long before—literally. The guests were at breakfast, and some sort of confrontation, resolution, denouement, whatever seemed about to take place. But the tension was briefly relieved, as it is sometimes relieved in a play by Shakespeare when a pair of yokels score points off one another before the hero and his antagonist confront each other in the final scene. Just before the climax in the breakfast room, the student of form guides got up to leave—for the nearest race meeting, presumably. As she was leaving, one of the main characters detained her for a moment, perhaps offended by her detachment from the others and their concerns. He said something to her along the lines of 'Could you not say something kind to Cynthia in her time of turmoil?' or 'Surely you've sensed this morning the burden that Ralph has to bear?' My plain-faced heroine, for that's what she became for me as soon as she had delivered her reply, waved her form guides in the face of her questioner and said words to the effect of, 'Give me horses rather than people any day. Horses are so much more predictable!'

Many times, as a young man, I could have wished for no better way of life than was had by the woman punter in Rattigan's play. I could not imagine, perhaps, how I might be freed from the need to work for a living, but I could readily imagine myself doing without the distractions of a wife and family. In 1957, one of the things that woke me out of my brief daydream of becoming a priest was my realising that a feeling of closeness to a mental image of God would never sustain me through a lifetime as a celibate, and yet I was often confident during the next few years that I could do without a girlfriend or a wife if I was able to devote myself wholly to racing. I sometimes tried to weigh up the matter. I would ask myself what was the worst possible experience I could have as a bachelor-racegoer. My most common answer would be that I could think of nothing worse than arriving home after a day of heavy losses—arriving home to an empty flat and having to prepare some sort of meal. But then I would argue that the misery to be endured in such a situation was by no means worse and probably rather less than the misery of learning that a young woman I had been interested in for some time was not in the least interested in me.

The horsey woman in Rattigan's play had not smiled when declaring that she found it easier to forecast races than human behaviour. Nor am I smiling when I write that I got from horse racing during the first twenty-five years of my life more than I ever got from any friendship or courtship. My wife and I were together for a few months less than forty-five years, and I could never doubt today that each of us had a better life than if we had remained single, which had been something of a possibility for both of us when we took up together in our late twenties. Even so, there were weeks and months during those forty-five years when I could not have brought myself to write a sentence such as the previous.

During most of the countless hours that I've spent on racecourses, I've been alone. And yet I've never once felt awkwardly or conspicuously alone at the races as I used to feel at dances or parties or holiday places. If, as a young man, I found myself in the company of an attractive young woman in a place other than a racecourse, I would be at first distracted and afterwards annoyed that I was prevented by a thousand obstacles from knowing more about her. If I came up against the same young woman on a racecourse, I would barely glance at her before getting on with my business and would feel no less a man for having behaved thus.

From my earliest years as a racegoer, there were numerous women among the spectators but few among the participants. For many years, all trainers and jockeys were men, as were most owners. I don't even recall seeing female strappers for many years.

Bookmakers were all men and so, too, were most of the throng in the betting ring. No solitary male could ever feel out of place on a racecourse. The men around him might have been lechers or satyrs on other days, but on race days they had the appearance of an order of celibate friars or monks following a religious rule or a motto like that of St Benedict: *Work and pray!*

There were also, of course, genuine bachelors, especially among my extended family or other Catholic families of their acquaintance. I was often at the races during my early years with my bachelor-uncle Louis. We sometimes met up with the Goonan brothers, Louis's cousins on his father's side. The Goonans were a family in which the majority of the siblings never married. Dan and Louis Goonan raced horses under the colours Pink, gold cap. My father warned me against the Goonans. He said they were mean and narrow-minded. I strongly suspect that they once turned my father down for a loan, which is what anyone in his right mind would have done. The Goonans *were* stingy, and I disliked them for it, but I admired their stern, celibate way of life.

On the day before the two-day summer meeting at Warrnambool in, I think, the late 1950s, a car travelling from Melbourne to Warrnambool was struck by a train at one of the level crossings on the Princes Highway. The two people in the car were killed. In those days, such accidents were by no means uncommon. Level crossings, even on the busy highway, were marked only with painted wooden posts or with white markings on the road. I might mention here an accident that happened once near Allansford, at Grauers Crossing, one of the most dangerous. A travelling salesman driving alone was struck by a race train on its way back to Melbourne after a

Warrnambool meeting. Perhaps I've written sometimes in this book as though racegoers are a mostly virtuous lot or that racing brings out the best in people. If so, then I'll do well to report here that the salesman's suitcases full of samples and supplies, whatever they were, were flung along the railway line after the crash. The train, of course, had stopped. The driver of the car died soon afterwards at the scene, but before he died he pleaded in vain with the dozens of home-going punters who had jumped down from the carriages and were picking up and pocketing the scattered goods.

The first of the two accidents mentioned above was reported in the *Warrnambool Standard* on the following day, which was the first day of the two-day race meeting. The two persons killed had been a man and a woman, both in their fifties. The man was named Rupert Taylor. I've forgotten his middle name. He was described as being a racehorse trainer from Dover Street, Flemington.

Rupe Taylor, as I once heard my father call him, was one of the numerous small-time trainers who struggled then and still struggle today to earn a living from racing. I can never recall any of Taylor's small team winning, although he must surely have won some country races during the time while I was aware of him. I found his colours distinctive and pleasing. They were Orange, red hoops and cap, and I would have liked to commend whoever had designed them. I had never seen Taylor, but when I read of his death I formed an image of a smallish grey-haired man. He was smallish because, like so many trainers then and now, he had formerly been a jockey. He was grey-haired, of course, because he was in his fifties, which for someone of my age at the time seemed old. Taylor had two horses engaged at the Warrnambool meeting. Many another small-time trainer might have towed his horses in a two-horse float but Rupe's horses got safely to Warrnambool, I gather, because they were sent in the care of a horse-transport company. I can't recall whether the horses were scratched or whether, as sometimes happens in such a situation, another trainer saddled them up or was even asked by the owner to take them into his stable.

Dover Street, Flemington, was unknown to me in the 1950s and I would have had no access for some years to a street directory that could have told me the whereabouts of Taylor's stables. I've written earlier about what I think of as Old Flemington. Dover Street is very much a part of Old Flemington. Taylor almost certainly lived in a plain-looking weatherboard house with six or eight horseboxes in the backyard. I can see the yard now. On a wet day, the bluestone paving is sloppy with horse dung. On a hot day, the air is full of yellow chaff specks. A drooping pepper tree completes the image.

In the brief newspaper report of the level-crossing smash, the information about Rupe Taylor was followed by a single sentence: *Also killed in the crash was Mary Christian Murday of the same address.*

Nowadays, of course, people live with their partners or with their fiancés or fiancées, or their boyfriends or girlfriends, or they simply live together. For the umpteenth time in this book, I have to remind the younger reader that things were quite otherwise during the Great Age of Racing. Mary Murday was lucky not to have been described as the *de facto* wife of Rupe Taylor or as his common-law wife. A decade earlier, the newspaper report would have omitted the addresses of the dead couple so as not to offend a certain sort of reader by reminding him or her that some persons cohabited without benefit of clergy, to use another expression of long ago.

I was strangely affected by the few words that I read about Mary Christian Murday, and I've thought of her from time to time during the sixty years since. I mean that I've recalled the image that I formed long ago of a quiet grey-haired woman of no particular distinction: someone who would pass largely unnoticed on a racecourse. Nothing that I wrote in the previous sentence has any justification in fact. For all I know, Mary was a tall, overpowering woman who wore much make-up and large hats and had a loud, grating voice. And yet, I can never think of her in that way. If I had read that Mary was Rupe's wife, I would have forgotten her and him a few months later and this book would have had one less section. But Mary and Rupe were not married. Two such persons nowadays would seem to me mere followers of fashion. It takes no special quality to be a follower of fashion—to live nowadays with your boyfriend or to have been sixty years ago a Sunday-school teacher insisting on a church wedding. Mary and Rupe followed no fashion. They acted, as a quaint old expression of my childhood would have put it, according to their lights. By doing so, they and a few others of their kind upended the fashions of their day as a few unknown and unknowing persons may eventually upend our own fashions, unthinkable as it seems to us.

For whatever reason, I found the courtship and marriage customs of my time cruel, even barbaric. Someone of my nature might say the same about the courtship and marriage customs of any age. Even so, I have sometimes wished I could have met up with Mary Christian Murday before her untimely death. I have sometimes supposed that Mary might have had a daughter of my own age. The young woman's father would have been not Rupert Taylor but someone, almost certainly a racing man, who was now out of sight and mind. As a result of some unimaginable set of circumstances, I would have been visiting Rupert's stables on an afternoon in spring, when the pepper tree was waving in the north wind. Mary, in her quiet way, would have introduced me to her daughter, who would have been by no means unlike her mother.

25. Reward for Effort

MY WIFE, AS I wrote earlier, took no interest in racing except when she was actually at a meeting. Then, she would become absorbed in the form guide. I considered her selection methods unsystematic and haphazard and was sometimes rude enough to tell her so, but Catherine had her share of successes. Towards the end of the previous century she began taking an interest in horses ridden by the young jockey Luke Nolen. She did this for no other reason than that Nolen was a cousin of one of her girlfriends from way back. If you follow any capable jockey, you'll get your share of good-priced winners, and Nolen brought Catherine just enough success to justify her sticking with him.

Early in the present century, Nolen became the jockey of first choice for the up-and-coming trainer Peter Moody and Catherine's strike rate, as they call it, improved considerably. She and I had been regular racegoers for fifteen years by then, and we could not have known that we had only two or three years left before she would be too frail to get to the races. During those two or three years, however, the combination of Moody and Nolen sent her home in a good mood on many a Saturday.

Catherine, who had been a heavy smoker for all of her adult life, was found to have untreatable metastatic cancer in May 2008. The cancer would have begun in one of her lungs at least a year before but had moved to a number of other parts of her before it was found. The young doctor who told this news to Catherine and me one afternoon in the Austin Hospital was flushed and trembling from nervousness. I guessed that the other members of the medical team treating Catherine had sent her to Catherine's bedside as a sort of learning experience. I wonder what the doctor had been expecting. I wonder what she made of Catherine's and my response to the news. Catherine said, quietly and almost to herself, 'So, I'll be dead soon…' She sounded almost relieved. She had by then lost the use of a leg from nerve degeneration, possibly caused also by her heavy smoking. I said to her, calmly also, 'Well, at least you're not going to end up in a nursing home!' We had been dreading this possibility for some time past.

No one would tell us what Catherine's life expectancy was. She and I suspected that she had about four months after the first diagnosis, meaning that she should have died in September 2008. In fact, she lived for twice that length of time, and was in and out of hospital half a dozen times. When Catherine was first in hospital, the social worker predicted that my wife would have to spend the remainder of her life either in hospital or in a nursing home with special facilities for caring for the terminally ill. Catherine certainly spent much of her remaining time in hospital, but during the rest of the time she was at home, with me for her nurse. She had regular visits from palliative-care nurses, but mostly I did everything for her. Why wouldn't I? I was fit and healthy myself, and I knew more about her medical history than any of her many doctors and nurses.

I kept a detailed diary of everything that happened to Catherine during her last eight months. I learned from that diary, after everything was over, that I had spoken during those months with more than thirty doctors and more than a hundred nurses. I've forgotten most of them by now, but when I last looked through my diary I did a rough tally and estimated that about a quarter of both the doctors and the nurses had seemed either lazy or incompetent. Two doctors and a few nurses seemed to be halfwits. At the other end of the scale, I met a few doctors and not a few nurses that I would have trusted with the care of my own life.

The best nurses were from the Royal District Nursing Service. Not one of them could be faulted. They visited Catherine every few days, not just to wash her but to check out numerous matters. Most of them said little to me or even to Catherine. One was an exception. While she was washing Catherine one day in the bathroom with the door closed, I thought I heard her, the nurse, telling Catherine something about the spiritual world. Afterwards, I asked the woman directly: had she been preaching some kind of sermon to my wife?

She was an interesting woman, this nurse. She had no rings on her fingers and seemed to be the sort of person who had never been interested in men. In answer to my question, she was immediately on the front foot. Too many doctors and nurses, she said, treated their patients as though they were bodies only. She, this aggressive nurse, was ready, unless her patients objected, to offer them comfort by talking of the spiritual world that surrounded the material world. She was even ready to assure them that the spiritual part of them would survive their bodily death.

I let her talk. I was more intrigued than she could have known. She had not much more to tell me. It concerned a dear friend of hers who had died of cancer. The friend had been a woman, and had promised to send a sign from the spiritual world, if such a thing turned out to exist. The dying woman and her dear friend, my informant, had agreed on what the sign should be. My informant was no idle gossiper. While she was telling me this she was making entries in her diary and completing other paper work. She was at my front door when she delivered her punch line. 'I got my sign,' she said. She was already on her way to the front gate when she gave me her parting message: 'I got exactly the sign I had asked for,' she said. 'The spirit world is out there. It's all around us.'

If the woman had not been a non-stop nurse and teacher, I might have had an opportunity to tell her that my wife and I had already made the sort of pact that she, the nurse, and her dear friend had made. Catherine and I had both been brought up in the Catholic Church but had later lapsed, as they say. I had lapsed many years before she, and yet by the time when she was dying she seemed to believe in nothing, whereas I would have shared the beliefs of the outspoken nurse.

I wrote in an essay that was later published in my book *Invisible*

Yet Enduring Lilacs that a writer such as myself would probably cause less offence to readers and scholars if he confessed to being a sexual deviant than if he confessed to believing in a world of the spirit—to being other than a materialist. I hereby confess that I have never been a materialist. I have no belief in any gods or angels or demons, but I have believed all my life in an invisible world of the spirit.

I mentioned a pact between my wife and myself. It should probably not be called a pact, because Catherine never actually agreed to it. I suggested it to her often, and long before she was diagnosed with cancer. She always responded with silence. I took this to mean that she would take part in the pact if it proved to be possible but that she would prefer to wait and see. The terms of the pact, or whatever it should be called, required the first of us to die to arrange for the survivor to back, on the first Saturday after the other's death, a winner at odds of twenty-to-one. When devising the terms of the pact, I had given much thought to the matter of what the winner's odds should be. To have asked simply for a winner would have proved nothing. To have asked for a winner at twenty-five-to-one or even longer odds seemed to be asking too much. I had never kept statistics, but I would have estimated that a twenty-to-one winner occurred about once in every month at a Saturday meeting, or once in every thirty races. Of the horses that contested those races, about sixty might have been at odds of twenty-to-one. But the person who had to fulfil the pact from the spirit-world was not only required to arrange for a once-a-month event to take place in a particular week—he or she had to make sure that the twenty-to-one winner was a selection of the survivor.

Catherine died on the Thursday before the Blue Diamond Stakes at Caulfield in February 2009. I could have made her task vastly more achievable if I had spent Blue Diamond Day backing only horses at twenty-to-one, but that would have been cheating. I made her task difficult indeed. For some years past, I had been following a select list of horses. I had their names in a ledger— two hundred of them, in several states. They were mostly younger horses with good form. I added two to my list each week and removed two that had disappointed me in recent months. I bet fifty dollars win-only on the tote on every one of my horses at every one of its starts. In the previous five years, I had twice earned a small annual profit. In the other three years, I had lost only very small sums. So, on the first Saturday after Catherine's death, I was committed to backing the horses that I would have backed in any case, even though none of them might have been at double-figure odds, let alone twenty-to-one.

About twelve of my select list of horses were engaged on the crucial day. I had starters in several states of Australia, but the only one likely to start at about twenty-to-one was in the Blue Diamond Stakes itself, the rich race for two-years-old horses. Because I kept many smart two-years-old horses on my list, I had to back four in the Blue Diamond. I've forgotten the names of three of the four but not their odds. One was the warm favourite, which was trained at Flemington by Steve Richards and had dark-blue and orange colours. Another was at about ten-to-one. Still another was at about forty-to-one. The name of the fourth of my horses is the title of this section. When I backed the horse, it was showing about sixteen-to-one on the tote.

I wrote somewhere far back in this book that I'm not a mumbo-jumbo man. Before the Blue Diamond, I made sure to tell my friend David Walton about the pact that I had tried to arrange with Catherine. David once told me that he had been an atheist and a materialist since his early childhood. I didn't tell him about the pact in order to convert him. I merely thought I should have at least one witness if anything significant happened that day. I have no recollection of anything that happened in the Blue Diamond Stakes of 2009 until the field was well into the straight. I was not tense or anxious on account of my two hundred dollars that was riding on the result, but I felt as though something of enormous consequence was about to be decided. My hands could not keep my binoculars steady.

My first recollection is of Reward for Effort (White, red logo and cap) leading by several lengths at the top of the straight. Next, I saw the favourite, in the dark blue and orange, urged forward in pursuit of the leader. People who have watched races for decade after decade learn to be acute judges of comparative speeds of horses and to estimate precisely the outcomes of races long before the contestants reach the post. I understood at once that the favourite was going to win comfortably. I had not forgotten that I had backed the favourite. If it won, I would have got back most of my outlay on the race. But money was not my concern. During the last minute before the race, I had learned that the odds against Reward for Effort had lengthened somewhat. As the horses approached the two-hundred-metre post, I felt a strange dismay. I felt as though Catherine had tried but had failed. Or, worse still, I felt a fool. The universe itself was mocking me.

The results of the Blue Diamond Stakes show Reward for Effort as the winner. The stewards reported after the race that the favourite had choked on its tongue in the straight. I recall nothing whatever of Luke Nolen's bringing his mount back to the winner's stall or of Peter Moody's greeting them. I don't even recall my collecting my thousand dollars and more, but I'll never forget that the winner paid twenty dollars and a few cents.

26. *They're Racing in the Antipodes*

I VAGUELY RECALL a comedy routine from the years before television, which were, of course, the years of radio. It was probably a recording that was played occasionally on one or another radio station. The subject matter was a mock radio program. Ads, songs, news items, and much else went forward rapidly. No doubt the stuff was mildly humorous and satirical, but I heard it seldom and I've forgotten all except the announcer's frequently interrupting proceedings with a short, sharp statement. The first words were always, 'They're racing...' What followed was at first mildly provoking: '...at Alice Springs' or '...at Oodnadatta'. One of the later statements is still quoted sometimes today by persons who probably never heard the original context but who enjoy the euphony—'They're racing at Manangatang.' As I recall, the last such statement, near the end of the whole program, was 'They're racing on Mars.'

I suppose the statements I've quoted might sound mildly amusing even today to persons who haven't the least idea of the origins of them. Very occasionally, during my childhood, I might have heard some or another actual program interrupted by a radio announcer's telling us that a race had begun far away. In truth, however, no radio station ever bothered its listeners with reports of races having started at remote venues. Not for the first time some clever scriptwriter had betrayed his or her total ignorance of horse racing.

I've mentioned previously the importance of illegal SP betting in the Great Age of Racing. Those radio stations that once broadcast races—and there were many more then than nowadays—might sometimes have confronted the problem of two races from different venues being about to clash. This would have often occurred during the years before starting stalls were introduced and when fields sometimes spent five minutes or more preparing to jump away. As a service to SP bookmakers, those radio stations would have announced sometimes that a race had begun at Ballarat, let's suppose, while the field at Flemington had still not been dispatched. Bookmakers betting on the Ballarat race would have been warned to take no further bets. Communications were comparatively primitive then, but perhaps someone might have learned by telephone the result of the Ballarat race and might have backed the winner with an SP bookmaker if the radio station had not made their announcement.

So, no one in my part of the world ever heard the dramatic-sounding statement that a field of horses was just then on its way at some faraway location. And yet, when I was searching for a title for this section of my book, I could think of nothing more appropriate than a comic radio routine from sixty years ago.

The comic routine, as I called it, brought to mind a world in which horse races are an ever-present background. No everyday action can go forward without being interrupted by the news that a race is in progress somewhere. This might seem a fanciful situation to many people, but it seems to me a strangely accurate description of what has been going on in my mind for almost as long as I can remember. At an early age, I became aware that a far part of my mind was the setting for a sort of endless race meeting. I seem to have accepted this with no fuss. I seem also to have learned very early that the glimpses of races that I saw in mind or the snatches of race broadcasts that I heard in mind were *not* derived from actual races that I had seen or had read about or had heard broadcast on the radio. Details of the image-races, so to call them, were not always clear but I understood that they took place on no racecourse that I had ever seen or read about. The site of my image-races was more remote, in a sense, than Manangatang or Mars. The names of my image-horses, even when I heard them clearly, belonged to no horses that I knew. The racing colours, what I could see of them, were all strange to me.

The turf, as Jack Kerouac once wrote, was so complicated it went on forever. Nowadays, races are run on seven days of the week in Australia. Not only that, but specialist television channels and the internet provide coverage of races in numerous countries overseas, and a person can watch and can bet on some or another race at almost any hour of the day or night. Things were nothing like so hectic in my boyhood, but I still heard or read about races interstate as well as three or four meetings each week in Victoria. And yet, the abundance of actual racing seems never to have been enough for me, to the extent that I was driven to imagine my own private racing world. But perhaps I didn't imagine it. Perhaps what I've been seeing in mind and hearing in mind all these years are details from an alternative universe. Do physicists and astronomers allow for the possible existence of alternative universes? Or, did I pick up the phrase from my non-racing friend Bruce Gillespie, who used to talk to me at length in the 1970s about science fiction?

One day in 1985, I sketched a map of two large bodies of land separated by a comparatively narrow strait but otherwise surrounded by a vast ocean. The more northerly of the two is not unlike the North Island of New Zealand; the more southerly resembles an enlarged Tasmania. The more northerly is named New Eden; the more southerly is New Arcady. Each is an independent nation with a political status similar to that of Canada in the Commonwealth, but the two use the same currency and are separated by no customs barriers. Each has its own tricolour flag and its own national anthem—'Oceans foaming...' for New Eden and 'In the shade of the world...' for New Arcady. The two countries are often referred to collectively as the Antipodes. The universe of which they are part differs from our own only in that the entities known to us as Australia and New Zealand have no existence in it.

I don't recall my feeling any strong urge or compulsion while I drew the coastlines of my two countries or while I afterwards marked on my maps the mountain ranges, the rivers and lakes, the cities and towns, and the highways. I felt more a sense of relief and also of expectation. I would soon know at last and for certain the names of the horses I had seen as flickering mental images for most of my life. I would soon know the names of their trainers and jockeys. I would soon know the exact details of the racing colours carried by each horse. I would know the names and the shapes of the courses where my flickering races were run. I would know all these things and more.

I could not do things by halves while I was recording the background of my image-racing. Today, the details of horse racing in the Antipodes are recorded in a dozen folders containing nearly four hundred pages of information, including maps of the forty-two racecourses in the Antipodes. Six hundred race meetings are held each year in the Antipodes, and one of my folders lists the date of each meeting and the major races for each. Other folders include the names and the colours of the fifteen hundred full-time and part-time trainers in the two countries. (These are not the only colours described in my folders. I've recorded so far the colours of more than a thousand owners who prefer not to use the stable colours but to design and register their own.) Several hundred jockeys are listed. I could go on.

The items mentioned in the previous paragraph are stored in the upper drawer of a two-drawer filing cabinet. In the lower drawer are records of the horses themselves and of the races so far run in each of the two countries. For most races, results only are recorded, but for each of about one in ten races, I record not only the results but also the position of each horse at intervals throughout the race. Even recording no more than starters, riders, trainers, odds, and results can take several hours for the one race; calculating the position of each horse at intervals takes three or four times as long. So far, only seven hundred races have been reported in my folders. (Any reader wanting to know how the details of races are calculated is referred to the piece 'The Interior of Gaaldine' in my book *Emerald Blue*, which was published by McPhee Gribble in 1995.) I should have added that about two and a half thousand horses have been so far entered in what I call my All-Horses Index, which lists every horse to have raced in the Antipodes and every one of its starts.

I've written in the above paragraphs about as much as I care to write at present about my Antipodean Archive, as I call it. Anyone wanting to know more will have to wait for a few more years yet. Anyone wanting to know, for example, how Strollaway (trainer T. D. Ivil, rider H. T. Holloway, colours White, grey quartered cap) came to beat Vicious Circle (trainer F. A. Ison, rider R. E. Middle-miss, colours Red, fawn hooped sleeves, white cap) in the Devonport Gold Plate, the richest race in New Eden and in the Antipodes, and how Vicious Circle, three months later, won the New Arcady Cup, the richest race in New Arcady, will have to wait until after my death and then to ask the executors of my estate whether any library was interested enough to acquire what I call my three archives.

The two-drawer filing cabinet mentioned earlier is not my only filing cabinet—far from it. I have also six four-drawer filing cabinets that I call my Chronological Archive. The twenty-four drawers of this archive are packed with thousands of letters and with diaries, autobiographical writing, and memorabilia from the past sixty years. The third archive is the Literary Archive. This consists of fifteen filing-cabinet drawers—one for each of the books that I've written: twelve so far published and three still unpublished.

My wife seldom intruded on me when I was at my desk of an evening, and I had been working on and off for nearly ten years on the Antipodean Archive before I first showed it to her. She did not look into the details, but she expressed her admiration for the whole and she left the room wondering aloud how I could have found the time to put such a thing together. If she had put the question directly to me, I could have answered it, but perhaps she knew me well enough not to need to ask. I could have answered by reminding her that I hardly ever watched television or listened to radio; that I watched hardly any films; that I had decided in early middle age that most books were not worth reading and that most music was not worth listening to or, at least, that I had read all the books likely to influence me and had heard all the music likely to affect me. Or, I could simply have reminded her that for most of my adult life I had devoted all my free time to minding my own business, in the truest sense of that expression.

27. Lord Pilate and Bill Coffey

BY 1988 I had been working for almost ten years as a teacher of creative writing in a college of advanced education. My job was satisfying and well paid, but, of course, it had its hardships and drawbacks. One minor hardship was that the college did not observe as any sort of holiday two of the most important days on the racing calendar: Melbourne Cup Day and the Labour Day holiday in March, when the Australian Cup was run. I usually managed to arrange my timetable so that I had no classes on Tuesday afternoon and could get home early to watch the Melbourne Cup on television, but that required me to take classes on most of Monday, so that I was usually in class when the Australian Cup was run. On Australian Cup Day in 1988, I had a window of opportunity, as they say. The Cup was going to be run during an hour when I was free of classes.

This was especially pleasing because the Cup that year promised to be one of the best races of its kind for many years. Two outstanding horses were going to clash in the race: Vo Rogue and Bonecrusher. There were other good horses in the race, but tipsters considered it a match between the two. (Vo Rogue's colours were Brown and white; Bonecrusher's were Brown and cream.)

Early in the day, I went to the room where we stored television sets, technology for language laboratories, and other devices that I could not even have named. (That might have been the time when the first computers were finding their way into our institution and I made my fateful decision to have nothing to do with them.) Anyway, the man in charge of all the technical stuff told me I was welcome to use one of the television sets for a few minutes later in the day. I learned from our brief conversation that he had never heard of the Australian Cup and that I was the only person on the whole campus to have approached him with my sort of request.

A few minutes before the Cup, I went to the technical room, or whatever they called it, and tuned in my set. I had thought I might find a few other people waiting for the big race, but I was alone in the room. I felt more than ever before that I was an outsider in my place of employment. I had hardly ever been into the staffroom at morning teatime or at lunchtime. This was mostly because I was usually too busy preparing for my many classes or assessing the many assignments that my students wrote, but also because I could seldom join in the conversations among my colleagues. They talked often about what they called *issues*. A typical conversation arose when someone asked, 'Who saw that documentary about such-and-such last night on the ABC?' And then, away they went, each vying to give his or her opinion. Or, if it wasn't a television documentary, it was politics. If they talked about sport, it was either football or cricket or, perhaps, tennis. Maybe they talked about racing at Melbourne Cup time, but I was never around to have to listen to their inanities. As I've said, I was hardly ever in the staffroom and, while I waited for the Australian Cup, my colleagues seemed more remote from me than ever.

I was still alone when the field for the Australian Cup was being loaded into the barrier stalls. Then I heard someone enter the room behind me—followed by someone else. So, I was not the only one on the whole campus who could appreciate horse racing! When I looked around, I saw the Buildings Officer, whose name I've long since forgotten, and a young man I knew only as Jason, the gardener's apprentice. (Dandy Andy, carrying Black and yellow squares, green cap, beat the two favourites in the race, but that's another story.)

It was not only among my tertiary-institute colleagues that I felt out of place. I haven't lacked for friends during my life, but I've never belonged in any circle or group. For much of the 1970s, my wife and I mixed from time to time in a group that included a writer or two, a few academics and teachers, and a few people connected with the theatre. They were mostly witty people, and we often fell about laughing. I can't recall ever being bored in their company, but perhaps that's because I always drank a lot. They might have been fun to be with, but I never felt close to them. I'd had two books published by then, and the people I'm talking about seemed to have assumed that because I was a writer I was like them in having left-wing political beliefs, reading the *Age* and tuning in to the ABC. Sometimes, I liked to provoke them. Sometimes, after

I had drunk a good deal, I used to argue that horse racing had as much to teach us as had Shakespeare and certainly much more than some of the pretentious films and plays that they were fond of praising and discussing. They mostly assumed I was joking, but sometimes they gave me a hearing, and one night I tried to tell them how I had been affected by what I had seen of the owner-trainer Bill Coffey.

I knew very little about Bill Coffey. I had surmised a few details, and I imagined others. Bill was a New Zealander, but I didn't even know what district he came from. He had first arrived in Australia in the mid-1960s with his horse Straight Irish (Purple, gold band and cap, red sleeves). Bill had brought the horse to Australia at least twice, with moderate success. Straight Irish had won only one race in Melbourne but had earned prize money from several placings in relatively rich races and had run fifth in Polo Prince's Melbourne Cup at odds of two-hundred-to-one. I tried to explain to my not-very-receptive audience how I much preferred to study the career of such as Bill Coffey than to watch, for example, any of the Greek dramas that they, my audience, might have watched and been moved by. I could never, I said, be affected by the sight of some actor's wailing and throwing her arms around after she had killed her children—I should have said her *pretend children*. Nor could I be affected by some actor's long soliloquy after he had copulated with his mother, daughter, whoever. (I had only a vague knowledge of Greek drama, but I thought I knew enough to make my point.) What *did* affect me, I said, and in this I was being wholly sincere, was the sight of a man such as Bill Coffey leading back towards the saddling paddock a horse that had come close to winning a big

248

race but had faded in the straight to earn only a minor prize. Bill, to judge from his dress and his appearance, was a humble man whose horse was his only means of acquiring wealth. The race just run had not ruined him. He was not at all crushed or impoverished. But Fate, through the agency of horse racing, was leading him on, teasing him, seeming to promise what it might never deliver.

I said this and more about Bill Coffey, and whatever my audience said in reply is no part of this story. They were certainly not converted, although I must have at least made sense to one of them.

She was a young woman, the girlfriend or wife of a man I have no recollection of. The pair were newcomers to the circle, having arrived recently from New Zealand. She had dark hair and pale skin, and I found myself looking often at her. She said nothing to me on the night when I preached my sermon about Bill Coffey but many months later, when she and her man and my wife and I happened next to be under the one roof, she took me aside and told me quietly that she had been back to New Zealand since she had last met up with me. She had made enquiries there about Bill Coffey and had learned a little. He had worked for most of his life in timber mills. She named a district of New Zealand but I, being half-drunk, never afterwards remembered it. Bill was a single man, whether a bachelor or a widower or divorced she did not know. His practice for many years had been to work in the timber industry for year after year until he had enough money to buy a horse likely to earn him a modest living. He would then give up his job and would train his horse full-time for as long as it could support him. After Straight Irish had been retired, so my dark-haired informant told me, Bill Coffey had gone back to timber work again.

I never saw the young woman again. Perhaps she went on mixing with the same set of people, but my wife and I drifted away. The 1970s were nearly over; our three sons were no longer children who could be put to bed in someone's spare bedroom while she and I partied on in the lounge room or the barbecue area. I had gone back to full employment, and our weekends were too precious to spend on bandying words with would-be intellectuals. I've never regretted losing touch with Barry Oakley and his court, but I still wish sometimes that I could have met up just once more in later years with the dark-haired young woman. I would not have spoken to her in the hearing of others but would have taken her quietly aside as she had once taken me aside and would have told her the last that I had ever learned of the story of Bill Coffey.

Bill came back to Melbourne one final time towards the end of the 1970s. Perhaps he brought more than one horse, but I recall only Lord Pilate. (His colours were the same as for Straight Irish; all Bill's horses carried the same colours.) Lord Pilate was aged eight or even nine and was a steeplechaser. He had won good races in New Zealand but struggled to find form in Melbourne. I knew that the Great Age of Racing had truly passed when the Victoria Racing Club, a few years ago, abolished jumps races at Flemington; at the time that I'm writing about, hurdle races and steeplechases were still run there. One Saturday at Flemington, a day of drizzling rain in the late 1970s, the horse Lord Pilate fell or was brought down in a steeplechase. The incident took place at a fence early in the straight. The field moved on to the winning post and afterwards slowed down, stopped, and were then walked back by their jockeys towards the mounting yard. Lord Pilate lay on the track where he had fallen.

He was alive but unable to get to his feet. Those in the grandstands who were aware of the situation understood that the veterinary surgeon would have been hurrying towards the horse to authorise its being put down, or euthanised, to use the acceptable term of our own times. Not only was the vet hurrying to the stricken horse—a team of track workers was on their way with a canvas screen that they would unfold and would place as a barrier between the horse and the grandstands while the vet was firing his bullet into Lord Pilate's brain.

A number of us in the grandstands stood with binoculars to our eyes, watching all this. We were not ghouls—far from it. We would all have had our own reasons for watching. Probably the most common motive was a wish to assure ourselves that the horse would have been put down as swiftly and mercifully as possible. And then, some of us would have become aware of something untoward appearing within the circumference of our magnified view of the far part of the Flemington straight.

The stricken horse, as I've said, was lying at the top of the straight. This was about four hundred metres from the mounting yard, where trainers, strappers, and owners would have been waiting for the contestants in the steeplechase to return. At some time while the horse, Lord Pilate, was still lying where he had fallen, a man was seen running towards the horse from the direction of the mounting yard. The man was making rather slow progress. He was wearing what my father used to call oilskins: a long, heavy raincoat reaching almost to his ankles. While the man ran, his coat flapped about him and hindered him, making him look like an ungainly or crippled bird. The man reached the fallen horse while the vet was still inspecting it and while the track attendants were still unfold-ing their screen. The man flung himself down onto the grass of the steeplechase track, beside the horse. The man put his arms around the horse's neck and pressed his face against the horse's head. The man went on lying there. The light rain went on falling. The vet and the track attendants stood without moving. They were not embarrassed. They were merely being respectful. They were horse-men too. They went on standing patiently. They went on waiting until the old man, the timber worker and part-time owner-trainer, had spent the measure of his grief.